Love

Value

Purpose

Love
Value
Purpose

BE LOVED. FIND VALUE. DISCOVER PURPOSE.

Amy R. Myers

Love ~ Value ~ Purpose
Copyright © 2021
Amy R. Myers

Publisher: Thy Name, Inc. (McLean, VA)

Cover Photo & Design: Grace E. Myers
Website: www.lovevaluepurpose.com
Contact: purpose@thy-name.com

Rights and Permissions: All rights reserved. No portion of this book may be reproduced, stored in a retrieval system, or transmitted in any form or by any means — electronic, mechanical, photocopy, recording, scanning, or other — except for brief cited quotations in critical reviews or articles, without prior written permission of the publisher.

The Holy Bible Permissions: All biblical passages from the ESV unless otherwise noted. ESV - PRINT - Scripture quotations are from the ESV® Bible (The Holy Bible, English Standard Version®), copyright © 2001 by Crossway, a publishing ministry of Good News Publishers. Used by permission. All rights reserved.

ESV - E-BOOK - Scripture quotations are from the ESV® Bible (The Holy Bible, English Standard Version®), copyright © 2001 by Crossway, a publishing ministry of Good News Publishers. Used by permission. All rights reserved. May not copy or download more than 500 consecutive verses of the ESV Bible or more than one half of any book of the ESV Bible.

NIV - Scripture quotations taken from The Holy Bible, New International Version® NIV® Copyright © 1973 1978 1984 2011 by Biblica, Inc. ™ Used by permission. All rights reserved worldwide.

NASB - Scripture quotations taken from the (NASB®) New American Standard Bible®, Copyright © 1960, 1971, 1977, 1995, 2020 by The Lockman Foundation. Used by permission. All rights reserved. www.lockman.org.

ISBN: 978-1-7368128-7-7 (Print)

Printed in USA

BLESSING

To those who search with wonder, longing, hope, and so much more, welcome to the journey ahead. May you discover and experience the reason and purpose for your search and how it can be deeply meaningful to your soul.

Contents

Chapter 1   Love ~ Value ~ Purpose 1

Chapter 2   Love: God's Voice 5

Chapter 3   Love: God's Care 9
                Savior Stories: Being Seen *13*

Chapter 4   Love & Value: Created 19
                Savior Stories: Don't Give Up *23*
                Savior Stories: Promises Kept *27*

Chapter 5   Love ~ Value ~ Purpose: Drawn to God 31
                Savior Stories: Desperate & Loved *38*

Chapter 6   Love ~ Value ~ Purpose: Experience God 43
                Savior Stories: Love. Sacrifice. Provision *51*
                Savior Stories: Healing Love *54*

Chapter 7   Value: Outside Influence 61
                Savior Stories: You Matter *71*

Chapter 8   Value: Inside Reset 77
                Savior Stories: Live to Tell *84*
                Savior Stories: Jesus Heals & Feeds *87*

Chapter 9   Love & Value: Forgiveness 89
                Savior Stories: For All He's Done *102*

Chapter 10   Purpose: Designed by Your Creator 107
                Savior Stories: Healed & Designed *116*

Chapter 11   Purpose: Loving Others as God Loves You 119
                Savior Stories: Help & Hope *127*
                Savior Stories: Women at the Resurrection ... *130*

Chapter 12   Love ~ Value ~ Purpose 135
                OPEN Your Heart to God *147*

1

Love ~ Value ~ Purpose

Love is described as many things in this ever changing world. The love of God is like no other and it is pure beyond human ability to match it. From this extraordinary love, we can truly understand everything we are designed to be.

In a world with hurt, pain, violence, and hate, how can we trust that God loves us? The injuries of our hearts are real. The wounding to our bodies and souls are significant. The intensity of pain, both physical and mental seem elevated in some chaotic, unexplainable way.

What are we as humans to do? What are we as sufferers or initiators of injury to do? There is pain and if we're honest, even as good people, we've caused pain to someone at some point in our lives. The injuries go from slight and forgettable to horrific images we cannot remove from our hearts or minds.

Life hurts.

For everyone.

Every person has a wound, usually many. Yet, we walk around like we are to put a smile on our faces, think positive and do something good, then magically these actions will create healing for the persistent feeling that something is not okay. Even our ongoing attention to the words of others and images to distract our minds can become places that add to our wounds and feel irrelevant to the struggles confronting our hearts and bodies with every breath.

Social media lets us pretend all is well. We share with the world what we hope doing well looks like. There's a twisted hope in the images and language spewed across the Internet with snippets and words of various apps. Twisted because looking good and feeling good become our standard for what we ought to feel inside or look like outside. The images display how pretty, strong, interesting, liked or accomplished a person can appear to be or how great their life is going.

Yet why are so many people increasingly filled with anger and hate, onscreen and elsewhere? The world seems to overflow with anger, lies and hatred. This cloud of anger oozes into so many parts of everyday life and it's splashed in our faces involuntarily. The toxic language mixes into the drive to hate and cancel anything or anyone. There's a strange desire to control or an evil laughter from the ones canceling someone. It creates a far-reaching destructive cycle of harm toward someone without a hint of acknowledgement that it's wrong.

So how can we even know what love is anymore? With a barrage of cloudy anger, where does the understanding of "love" fit and how do we figure out what that is? How do we go from toxic chaos to a place where our hearts and minds find peace and comfort? Can we feel as if there is goodness once again? Can we get to a place where you and I walk around knowing that love in its powerful, pure goodness, is a place we can rest our weary minds and hearts?

We're not describing romantic or idealized interpretations of what society declares today or tomorrow or at 2pm on any given day. It's not a moving target or opportunity for guessing as best as we can. Love that is pure, but also love that can be trusted.

It's precisely because of our twisted understanding of love, justice, or goodness that brings an urgent need to discover what the Creator had in His mind. God created our extraordinary planet and the far-away, mesmerizing places we can see captured on satellite imagery. This Creator precisely positioned this planet for our particular human bodies to comfortably exist in an ecosystem forever recycling itself in a cleansing, life giving way.

God did that and He knows what love is. He knows the extraordinary value of every person He created. He knows the purposes for your precise existence during this moment in history.

You are loved by God. He's willing to show you.

You are valued by God. He's willing to reveal this to you.

You have a purpose from God. He's willing to experience it with you.

Love. Value. Purpose.

2

Love: God's Voice

    This journey to understand love, value, and purpose begins with God and what some layers of His love looks like. We're going to try to imagine how that might feel. This may be a new type of experience for some, yet I encourage you to try. As you progress forward in this journey, you may want to come back to this chapter to see how you are experiencing changes while reading again the words that follow. Now, can you imagine yourself sitting in a room? It's a restful place and you're comfortable. You're purely happy in this place. Next, imagine a strong, good presence joins you and somehow you know it's God. He's not upset with you. You might be surprised, so you might wonder. Then, notice how His form radiates a bright, pure joy. Can you feel a great soothing peacefulness? Seeing Him, perhaps you wonder why He's with you.

Then, imagine you hear someone else speaking as you're sitting in this soothing presence of God.

> "In the beginning, God created heaven and the earth and all that is in it. He said it was good. All that He saw was good, especially those He made in His image...man and woman. The beauty extends beyond all you can imagine. And God made it for you. His heavenly realm is filled with greater beauty, but He wanted you to have the beauty of earth. Wholly given as a gift of His love. He's watched over it and all that is within it. It is precious to Him. All the people are precious to Him. He forgets not a one. He calls them by name and gifts them with favor and blessing. All the world sees the beauty God gave them. It is for joy, peace, provision, comfort, care, wisdom, and blessing."

Pause and try to bring to your mind and to hear as if in a dream of sorts, a gentle, loving voice coming from God. It carries soothing calm.

> "I do not gift lightly or insufficiently. I am God Almighty who chooses to bring loveliness. My love is great, and many try to cheapen it or lie about it. I am God who greatly loves and gives. I will not be deterred from my people. I love them and I am coming for them. They belong to me and not the evil in this world. I declare My presence will matter to them again. Holy, holy, holy. Honor and glory to the Lord. My people shall once again see the goodness of the Lord. I love them and I will come for them."

Then, as if you're hearing this with your heart:

"The Lord seeks to make right the sorrows of the hearts of many. The wounds inflicted by so many, on so many. God brings justice and hope. God provides goodness to the weak. God provides grace to the waiting. God pursues those lost like stray sheep. Those who need care and rescue. Worthy are they who seek Me. I am coming for you. Look to Me. I will come quickly.

"'Be not delayed,' they will shout. And for a time, it seemed a delay, but now is the time for my beauty to shine once again. Glory will come because I love my people. Justice will be mine for the weak and needy.

"Cherish the Lord who is the Savior. The Redeemer who came to save the world through His death and resurrection. Jesus healed the wounds, then and now. He heals today, for those who are called by Him and those who seek Him. They will be saved, healed and rescued.

"Be not worried for the Lamb of God loves you. He sees you. Embrace the Lord Jesus coming in the end. He will bring justice for the poor and downtrodden. He will heap gold on the wounded.

"Be at peace. Know I am still God. Be at stillness with Me, the Lord God. I will comfort you and heal you and be your Father. Honor God with your heart and being. Give love to God. Find love for others. Give love to all, especially the downtrodden. They wait and hope, but no one comes for them. They are weak, but no one comes for them. They are longing for God, but no one seeks them. Find them and bring them love. They are there. Help them. Be ready to help them.

"Love your neighbor as yourself. Be love and grace and kindness to others. Love God. Love others. Love with blessing upon blessing.

"Be not weary for my Spirit is coming.

"If you could love today, what would that look like? Where would it take you? Be free to pursue the desires I give your heart. Be ready to pursue them. The power is coming on the earth. I will manifest a great wind of fire and purpose. All that I am. I will bring mercy on people and save them."

The One who created the heavens and the earth stops speaking. He looks to you and knows it is almost too much to receive. Perhaps try to take a deep breath now, as God is simply asking that you let Him lead you to His heart. He wants to reveal a deep and great love for you. Continue on this journey and He will bless you with His love.

3

Love: God's Care

As we take this journey, we turn our pursuit to love. It's a something every one of us seeks, but it's hard to feel loved when you're told to look at all the things that aren't actually love. There are many declarations to be your "best self" that leave a person striving to make all the right choices or say all the right words. Others advocate a total denial of your individual existence as if we're fundamentally *desiring* to be bad people. These reject God's heart in two very specific ways. First, self-driven efforts will fail eventually, because God designed us to do life with Him in a personal way. Second, denying the extraordinary person God made (you) and lumping that in with our behavior tells God we don't think He created anything good. Our behavior does not remove the fact that what God creates is good.

These are truths God wrote on my heart through times of rejoicing as well as sadness. He guided my heart, mind,

Love ~ Value ~ Purpose

and soul to authentically love Him and to deeply accept the value He gave me. This matters for you too. To deeply know you are loved deeply matters to God.

The details of your life are different than mine, but God loves each of us with the same great love. God made us specifically unique so that in every relationship He has with each of us, the details matter to our very souls. There are places and crevices in our hearts that long for the presence of God, even though we usually don't know how much we actually crave it.

This personal pursuit of God's love became for me an unfolding journey with Him. God proved His true story of His love, value and purpose for you and me. Even with a new faith in God, I had no real understanding of the love of God. Unfortunately, this is common. This is true for those who know God generally and those who don't. So many can't find enough peace in their days to even wonder if they matter or if God could love them. There's an automatic thinking that we're not loved or even that we're unlovable. All the ways we've lived or how people treat us seem to tell our hearts that at best, we can be lovable as long as we behave the way others want or according to what's expected.

This happens in churches too. There are so many of us who think we're supposed to feel loved because we're at church. As if simply doing what's expected will make us lovable to God. But there is a severe lack of knowing and feeling loved all over the place. Happy faces and willing doers…these don't usually reveal the truth inside.

There are kind and compassionate people who give all of themselves to care for others in the work of God, and yet confess they don't know what the love of God feels like for them. Even women I know who lead Bible study groups and know a lot about the Bible have shared the same disbelief and don't feel personally loved. It's almost like we're not allowed to feel loved by God. We're only allowed to "love" others, but embracing that we are loved by Him is somehow selfish.

God loves us and that should be embraced. Loving yourself does not have to be a self-help, all-about-me concept. It's looking at God and seeing what He sees. God loves you and created you. Loving God is about loving all of Him, and that includes the beautiful treasures He creates. God created the heavens and the earth and all that is within it. People are His favorite part, and He loves His creation. Through God's eyes, we can begin to see ourselves as lovable just as we are. We can begin to see that God loves us simply because He made us.

We can begin to wonder how God personally loves us and what that looks like in the complicated lives we have. Even though many of us may respond, "Yes, God loves me," when someone asks, somehow many of us aren't entirely convinced. When pressed, many reveal to me that they don't really know what that means. Trying to follow a plan to read the Bible can give us the same void. Our questions may be, "How does this show me that I matter to God? He did that for all those people, but how does that show me He loves me today?"

The real discovery happens from how we pursue God and the words He shares in the Bible. Sadly, so many of us are guided away from this true discovery and we miss the power and compassion of God.

We can go beyond someone telling us, "God loves you," to experiencing God's love for us. We're built to experience God and He designed us to do exactly that.

God lovingly revealed this truth about His love in my life. God loved me when I didn't understand what that was. He healed my wounds and carried my weeping heart through trials. He gradually deposited evidence of His love in my life. God asked me to love Him, but He knew I didn't know how to love Him back..

God took the tiny seed of trust I gave Him and cultivated, watered, nourished and strengthened it. There were times I couldn't comprehend why the winds would come as a method to strengthen that trust. God taught me how to see that He was there with me. Discovering more about God from God is the only true way to begin to experience His powerful love.

We don't feel loved because we tend to think that trying hard enough and being good enough for as many people as possible will bring us the love we desire. We can see the brokenness it's brought to this world as we look at the anger, chaos and efforts at self-displaying one's "greatness."

To know you are loved, we need to go to the source of Who created love. It's how we're meant to live and how we're meant to be loved.

Love of the Savior Stories

As we travel this journey toward God, you will find brief stories at the end of the chapters titled Love of the Savior. God pressed on my heart the need to experience His stories as if we were there. These are true events, and the words Jesus speaks are directly from the Bible (ESV). The scenes are expanded by me to give us a sense of what it was like for the individuals experiencing the love and compassion of God. The biblical references show the place in the Bible where the story and Jesus' words can be found.

Love of the Savior

Being Seen with Compassion
Widow's Son
Luke 7:11-17

"I can't do this Lord. Not both of them."

The mourning crowd slowly walks with the weeping widow behind the procession of men carrying the wood plank. It's an open casket holding her only son, deceased. The women wrap their arms around the mother for comfort. She walks with a downcast head and mourning heart toward the city gates and burial grounds outside. The women know she's alone in so many ways. During the first century, a woman without property or protection of a husband or male heir could quickly become poverty stricken. As mothers and wives, they weep for her double loss of the most important men in her life. Heart-broken and unprotected.

The sounds of the procession are muffled to the widow's ears, distant and faintly surrounding her mind. The surreal covered body of her only son is the focus of her gaze, everything else is fuzzy. She barely senses the arms around her shoulders and back. Her relatives and neighbors walk with her in this darkest time. Her tears drip without notice or care anymore. Through streams of pain, she weeps deeply and silently in her soul.

"Lord, I just can't…"

Suddenly the procession stops. The widow forcibly blinks and slowly lifts her head. Her eyes focus on the men carrying her son's lifeless body.

She wonders, "Why are they stopping? What's happening?"

Confusion and reality begin to stir in her thoughts, alerting her eyes to pay attention. The sounds of people and crowds are loud and bustling as if she's finally hearing what's happening around her. She's realizing they're now through the city gates. A swarm of people move collectively toward the somber, emotionally isolated group of mourners. The widow watches as people begin to shift their gaze. She follows the collective eyes, faces, and bodies as the people begin to separate.

"Who's that man?" a whisper travels into her ears echoing her own thoughts.

The male figure in a linen tunic and sandals walks toward the mourners carrying the lifeless young man and the weeping mother. The separating crowd tracks Him with their eyes, then they step back slightly to let Him pass. The widow watches them, then her eyes drift to those of the man coming toward her. Peace and calm emanate from Him. There's something about His presence that pulls at her. It's a welcoming feeling, but she doesn't understand it. It's happening and she's merely experiencing it.

The man is in front of her now. He speaks to her gently. His voice carries compassion, and His eyes reveal His concern for the woman.

"Do not weep," He says looking directly into her eyes.

Trying to breathe and forcing her mind to translate what He says, she blinks. There's a calmness in her heart she doesn't recognize. The words linger in her and feel true somehow. The ache is briefly soothed. For this moment, the tears stop.

The peace-filled man shifts toward the son. The widow squints her eyes and slightly tilts her head. "What's he doing?" she questions silently, confused. "Is he going to touch him?"

The man looks at the body lying on the open wood plank, then He touches the casket. The men holding it stare in shock, overcome and still. The widow is in shock. The startled crowd surrounding Him stares. The bustling crowd and its noise are quiet now.

The man who gently spoke to the weeping widow is undeterred from the intensity of the crowd's emotions. They're confused and waiting, but unable to stop watching.

He says, "Young man, I say to you, arise."

The hush of staring people instantly changes as they wince and take in a breath. Their minds don't understand what their ears hear. This is not what any of them expected. What did He say to the dead body, the only son of the weeping widow?

For the widow, the moment seems as if she's in a slow-moving dream. The response of the crowd was the response of her mind but not her heart. It flutters and spurs toward hope. Her eyes shift away from the man who speaks and over to the son in front of her. Slowly she sees the covering begin to move. She watches as the dead man sits up. "My, my son is awake…," her thoughts shout as she tries to make it sound real in her mind. She watches her son look at the man with gentle eyes. The One who told her not to weep.

The man who brought life now helps the young man down from the plank used as an open coffin. The risen young man stands facing Jesus. The peace of the Son of God comforts the confusion of the once dead man. He feels the subtle pressure turning his body away and guiding him to the mother he saw when he had closed his eyes.

The widowed mother begins to reach forward. The One with gentle eyes leads the young man to stand before his mother. Her eyes see but her mind wrestles with disbelieving the images before her. Tears of thankfulness drip as the arms of her son embrace her with a strength she's known and remembers.

Her son is alive and in her arms.

There is no disbelief.

Jesus had seen her and had great compassion for her. He did this for them. As she holds her son, her heart gushes with a joy she's never known. Then she opens her wet eyes to look beyond the arms embracing her. She sees Jesus lovingly watching and peacefully acknowledging His gift to her. The widow feels the love of being seen and loved by this One who does miracles.

The widow's life is forever changed because of the Man she would come to know as Jesus the Savior. He had seen her, cared for her, and saved her son.

The crowd begins to change from paralyzing fear of what just happened to loud praise. They exclaim the glory of God. "God has visited His people!" the cheers proclaim.

As the cheers of people rise, the widow whispers to herself, "God, you heard me. You see me." She stands with her son as she absorbs the joy and awe of the people around her. She takes in the treasure of what just happened. She would always remember the One with gentle eyes who had compassion on her and changed her life.

Jesus is the One who saw the widow mourning the death of her son. He turned to care for her sorrow. The experience of seeing Jesus and being seen by Jesus is something powerful and unforgettable. The images and memories forever leave an imprint in those intangible places we describe as our hearts. The place where treasures can exist and cannot be taken away.

This can be our understanding of Jesus. Look at Jesus and you will see love. Pursue Jesus and let Him reveal how He treasures you. Look to God and you will begin to realize He's always seen you and has always loved you.

4

Love & Value: Created

"I have loved you with an everlasting love;
I have drawn you out with loving kindness."
— Jeremiah 31:3, NASB

The love of God is pure and can change our lives in extraordinary ways. To build a picture of love, we start at the beginning. God created the earth and all that is within it, including men and women, and it reveals His great love for all that He created. His greatest love is found in every person, because He created us as a reflection of His image. That's how God describes it. To protect those of us made in His image, He positioned earth in a precise location to provide for human existence.

The beauty, grandeur, and wondrous sites found throughout all of the world were placed here by the Creator to display His love and power. God is a loving God and created this display of goodness for His special creation, humans. It's for you to enjoy and to take in the love from the One who sent it.

All of us at some point are drawn to the beauty of the sky, mountains, waters, or beaches. Perhaps the desert or forests or the beauty deep within the oceans and seas. The vast display can feel as if it never ends if we truly ponder it all.

God created the earth for us. It's not for our selfish, hurtful ways, but it points us to Who created it. All the earth is designed to show us God and that He truly exists. His creation points to Him so we know He loves us and He's powerful enough to do great wonders that man cannot do. This is no simple display randomly occurring and coming into existence on its own. It's far too vast and complicated for that to be an honest idea. Parts of the earth change over time, but the grandeur was placed here. God didn't do it randomly. He did it for people because He loves what He created.

Can you imagine simply stating that the waters would exist, and it happens? This is God's power. That's what He does. He doesn't need the earth for Himself. He made it for people to enjoy and to observe with awe and wonder of its Creator. We can experience and see the seemingly endless number of places on earth He created.

God displays His love through creation for all to see. It's like an enormous advertisement to wonder more about who created such a masterpiece and why He created you to be a part of it.

Beyond the extravagance for everyone, God also intricately and uniquely places His imprint in you. God created the heavens and the earth, but He also created you. There are so many ways you are uniquely you. God designed you and knew every day of your life before you were born. For God, He sees all of time as one picture and you have a unique and precious reason God chose this time in history for you to be here. You are also part of a larger purpose that God has for you.

Part of God's imprints are wonderful ideas, abilities and passions He placed in you. He designed them to bring you unexplained joy when you experience them. That's God connecting His heart to yours. He planned that imprint and put it there. This intentional part of you is deeply connected to how you're designed to thrive. It's part of all the interesting details of how He enjoyed making you. We're designed by God to know Him, so He creates ways to draw us to Him.

Imagine a smile on His face every time you do something you've always loved since you were young. Maybe it's sitting on the beach as you listen and watch the gentle waves in front of you or the feel of water touching your feet. You may feel so peaceful and as if you were meant to be there. Or, perhaps you feel invigorated as you hike a difficult path up the mountain, strengthened to your core beyond the muscle strain. For some, it might be when you sing with young children as they learn something new in your kindergarten class. Your heart may feel as if it's bursting with joy being in the presence of curious little minds with great big hearts. Or maybe you love numbers and how they work together to tell a story or coded together to make electronic devices do fascinating things.

These are imprints. Your life has God's imprint, too. God placed passions and loves in your heart long ago, even though some may get pressed to the side as we do life. Others may have been brief joys or later in life discoveries. The key point is that God chose to place particular details in you that matter to your heart. When you have these experiences, you're tasting a little bit of what God lovingly chose for you.

His reason for placing something special in you that only He could do is so that you will know God is real and present in your journey. Too often we pass over these moments, experiences or passions and barely pay attention to them. They may not indicate life purpose or vocation, but they do reveal God's specific imprint designed to bring you, and especially you, His joy. God is showing you He loves you. How He's always loved you. It's how He "draws you out with loving kindness."

Love of the Savior

Don't Give Up on God
Daughter of the Synagogue Leader
Matthew 9:18-26; Mark 5:21-43; Luke 8:40-56

"Jairus, you must go. She's dying," the mother urges her husband.

"I don't know if He'll be there," the father says to his wife through his wet eyes.

She sits next to their only daughter, just twelve years old, dying. She touches the girl's forehead as the child lays still. Turning to her husband and reaching out her arm, she says "Come. Take my hand."

He had not let anyone else in the room, so they are alone. He holds his wife's hand. This leader of the synagogue tearfully looks at his wife and daughter, then squeezes her hand with the same desperation he sees in her eyes.

"Please go find Him. He's the only one who can save her," she pleads.

Kissing her hand, he promises, "I will find Him. I will do all that I am able."

As she watches her husband leave, she hears the sound of family and friends waiting for news of the girl. Trembling with tears, she mutters, "Lord, save her. Lord, please…" The ache in her stomach grows deeper and deeper. She weeps as the hands of her daughter grow cooler and cooler.

A relative steps to the edge of the doorway to see them, but tears drop from the woman's eyes and she can't bear to enter further. The sorrow of the weeping mother fills her heart as she watches the slow demise of the girl and the torment of her mother sitting beside her as it progresses. Leaving them, the girl appears dead. The woman knows the mother feels the death of her child, so she slips away to join the mourning family members outside.

The cries increase, especially from the women who have also held a dying child in their arms. Great grief. The immensely painful reality sets into the group of supportive loved ones.

The mother hears faint echoes of the crying, but she's afraid to leave this place with her daughter who is now different somehow. But as the startling reality reaches her mother's heart, the shock penetrates. Not knowing what to do, she stands and walks to the doorway and away from the death she senses.

Then, pulling her from her grief, she hears her husband's voice and the sound of people laughing. This is not a joyful laugh, rather a disbelief. "What's happening?" she thinks as she steps out into the daylight with the crowd.

The mother gasps when she sees them. Jairus and the One who must be Jesus. Her sadness tumbles around in her mind with possibilities. Her breath quickens as tears of hope well up. She blocks the sound of mocking relatives who challenge Jesus.

"Do not weep, for she is not dead but sleeping," the mother hears Him say to the people mourning for her daughter.

No one had ever seen death retreat and a life revived. Their disbelief comes out as laughing responses, reflexively not possible.

Jairus turns to look into the eyes of his wife. He'd been told on the way of his daughter's death, but Jesus came anyway. He remembered what Jesus had said to him. It's why he stood next to Jesus now, feeling differently.

"Don't be afraid; just believe, and she will be healed," Jesus had said on the way to Jairus' home.

The ruler of the synagogue believed Jesus, but not at first. Now, he stands with Jesus in front of his relatives who carry the disbelief he once had.

The mother watches as Jesus does not rebuke the crowd with anger. He simply encourages them not to weep. He motions for Jairus to go into the house. Then, Jairus walks up next to his wife and they enter. Jesus motions for three of His disciples to join them. There is no drama or display, but there is a sureness about Jesus. He stops the eager mourners and prevents them from going into the place where the girl lays.

Grabbing tightly to Jairus' arm, the mother holds on as they lead the men to their daughter. The girl's mother tries to control her breathing, but her eyes stay fixed on Jesus. His gaze only meets the eyes of the parents for a moment, then He turns to the girl. Every way He moves and walks is sure and peaceful.

Jesus steps next to the still body of the twelve-year-old girl. He reaches gently for her hand and lifts it. As He does, He speaks, "Little girl, I say to you, arise."

A gasp from her mother, whose lips quiver as she tightens her hold on Jairus. The hope of His words ricochets through every part of her.

The lifting of the girl's hand quickly becomes leading her. She sits up and gets off the bed.

Alive. Recovered. Healed.

And holding the hand of Jesus the Son of God.

Jairus and his wife are overcome with amazement and cry, "Oh Lord, thank you! Thank you!" Tears and trembling mix with wonder. All of it overflows from their hearts to their lips. The child rushes over to her parents and settles into a deep embrace.

Jesus watches the joy of the miraculous healing of the girl. Then, He encourages the parents to give the girl something to eat. The family of three pulls apart and looks at the Lord Jesus. Overwhelmed, but no longer in disbelief, they nod with the peace and joy of this moment tucked into their hearts and minds forever.

They would feed their only daughter to strengthen her, for Jesus wanted that for the child as well. They would celebrate and remember the day Jesus came to them, even when it seemed like it was beyond possible. The day Jesus walked from far away to raise their daughter from death.

Love of the Savior

Promises Kept
Anna Sees the Young Jesus
Luke 2:36-38

The woman carefully steps on the stones as she moves forward gingerly. Every step of her creaky old body takes effort. Every day she comes to this place, the stone fixture in Jerusalem. The Temple mount with great architectural stone walls and gate entrances leading to the sacred spaces where only the consecrated priests are permitted to enter the altar of the Lord. In the area where women and those coming to give sacrifices may walk, this is Anna's place of joy. A place of continued prayer and fasting since she lost her husband decades ago.

The crowds ebb and flow, and priests come and go. Faithful ones pray and pray, sitting before the God of Abraham, Isaac and Jacob. They pray and they watch. Anna is a prophetess and loves God. He's told her the day will come when the salvation of Israel will arrive.

From her many days of prayer, she met Simeon. He's a man of God, who comes here to offer prayer and thanksgiving to the Lord. Anna knows of the special promise God made Simeon. He would see the Messiah before his old body would give way to death.

"Lord, thank you for this day. Bless your great and holy Name," Anna prays silently as she nears the stone gates. The open square inside the gates is not terribly crowded today.

"May your servant hear Your voice this day and may my prayers honor You Lord," she whispers. Anna steps forward toward the shaded area where she often prays and rests her aging body. She scans the space and observes people as she moves.

Something comes into her range of vision. Simeon holds a child as he stands before what are obviously the child's parents. She shifts her feeble steps toward them. Simeon's face shows something new, something with joy. Anna scurries as quickly as her eighty-four-year-old legs would move.

Anna comes close and begins to remember the Lord urging her to "give thanks to the Lord and speak of Him to all who are waiting for the redemption of Jerusalem." Anna's heart begins to beat quickly. "Redemption of Israel," she mutters, "Could it be?" She can hardly imagine it after all these years.

She comes close to Simeon but doesn't interrupt. Anna wants to be within hearing range and to see more clearly. Simeon takes the child up in his arms and blesses God. Every move of his arms attaches to Anna's mind. The gentle wave of anticipation and peace careen through her body. She soaks in the feeling that the longing of her heart was becoming real. She had always hoped she would hear about it, but only dreamed that she might see the promises of God. She knew Simeon would. Anna hoped she might too. To be at the place where God begins to reveal a promise He made long ago. She knew it could happen and deeply wanted to be there when it did.

Anna knew the moment God had promised was here. She could see it in Simeon's eyes. His eyes sparkled with a knowingness only a fellow prophet understood. The Lord was also making it clear to her heart.

"He's holding a child. Lord, this is the One you promised. Here. Now. O Lord, merciful Lord!" she prays, taking it in with all her senses.

Simeon blesses the child and says, "Lord, now you are letting your servant depart in peace, according to your word; for my eyes have seen your salvation that you have prepared in the presence of all peoples, a light for revelation to the Gentile, and for glory to your people of Israel."

Anna takes in a full breath, absorbing the magnitude of his words deep within her heart. The Messiah lay in the hands of Simeon. As he brought his arms down, Anna noticed the couple. Their eyes are wide, even a bit overwhelmed at what was said about the child. Simeon blesses the family and gives a special blessing to the young mother directly.

The prophetess takes in every word, image and movement of the child. At that very moment, she feels God urging her to go to the parents. When they begin to walk away, Anna goes directly to them. She thanks God for this Child, who would redeem Jerusalem. It was a moment that God provided another public blessing for all He was doing for the world.

This day marked another promise God made to the world that He was keeping. He promised He would rescue His people in very specific ways to know it was Him. To Simeon and Anna, they knew this was the beginning of God keeping that promise to the world. They trusted God. God had also made a personal promise to Simeon and He kept it that day, too.

Anna treasured this gift God gave her. It meant a lot to her personally that she would witness the Messiah. She's loved the Lord all these years and cherishes His whispers to her as she prays and fasts in His Holy Temple arena. God gave this aging woman a most extraordinary gift. He knew her heart and that witnessing this moment was deeply meaningful to her. He did not need to include Anna in the announcement of the Messiah's arrival. The One who would save all humanity from eternal separation from God.

But God did. He chose to show His particular and meaningful love to Anna. God saw Anna and He loved her.

God sees you and those particularly meaningful elements of your heart, too.

God loves you. He will show Himself to you just as He showed Himself to Anna, the faithful woman who pursued and celebrated the great Creator and Redeemer God.

5

Love ~ Value ~ Purpose: Drawn to God

God draws you to Himself with love and kindness. He placed particular imprints of His design in you long ago. It lets you know God loves you, cares for you, and thought about you long before you knew what you would enjoy. Our internal and unique ways we are drawn to certain joys connects us personally to His love.

God also wants us to explore who He is in ways that are personal. God created the extraordinary heavens and wonders of the earth, but He also wants you to get to know Him beyond this magnificence. The One who abundantly loves the world and each person He created truly wants you to know more about who He is and why He made you the way He did. The Bible is one way God opens up stories of who He is and how He loves.

Part of our purpose is simply to get to know the One who created us. God designs it this way because He knows that the more time we spend with Him, the more we will experience His pure goodness and love. This pure love begins to push out all the unlovable harm that was thrown upon you in this broken world. You will feel the difference when you come close to Him. You can be healed and comforted. You can be revived and restored. God lovingly carries you toward replacing the wounds with love, joy, and peace.

The closer we get to God, the more we experience a soothing love and tender care for our souls. We all have wounds. God loves to heal those wounds if we will just give Him the chance.

As God presses out the muddy residue of life, our hearts can fill with a joy that rises unexpectedly. Then, we notice it along with peace and patience that we didn't have before and it makes our interactions with others different in a good way. It doesn't happen instantly, instead, it's something that grows in you and you begin to notice. The best part is that it's not you trying to be more peaceful or patient. God actually changes your heart from the inside, and you begin to experience what He's done for you. It's way more amazing than trying and trying to do better. God does the major work when we're willing to sit with Him to ask for His healing, and to see our situation the way He does. The best "self-help" is to get as close as we can to the One who truly helps us.

God carefully and lovingly revives us with His goodness. The more time we spend with God and really desire to know Him, the more of His peace and healing He will place inside of you.

Practically, what does this look like?

Honestly, the best way to start is to look around and ask God some questions. "God, I don't really know how to get close to you. Can you help me understand? I just know You are my best hope." The key is that God wants your heart trying to find Him and thinking about Him. It could be sitting down in a place without distractions and silently talking to Him. It could be singing to Him in the shower. You just have to want to be close to God and want to know who He truly is. To know God is to spend time with Him and reading stories about Him in the Bible.

When I was in college, I began to want to know God. My family members didn't believe in God and I wasn't raised going to church. Something began to stir in my heart and made me wonder about God. (By the way, that's God's Holy Spirit putting that longing in you for God). Then, as God sweetly does, He showed me that He saw lonely little me. I somehow found a Bible in the basement storage area and took it to my room.

I sat on my bed with this black Bible and said, "What's that thing people pray…Our Father, something, something."

That was all I knew about God and I must have heard people say it, because our family didn't talk about God. What I had been trying to find is known as the Lord's Prayer. I didn't realize that, but only knew it had something to do with God. For those who have never held a Bible, it has thousands of pages. I casually began turning those pages. After just a very short time of flipping pages randomly, there it was. At the top right of a page I saw, "Our Father, who is in Heaven…"

This particular passage is not at the beginning or the end in some convenient place. It's past the middle and not in a neatly highlighted part of the Bible. God opened that Bible and helped my eyes see the only thing I had ever known specifically about God.

That was the beginning of my journey to find God. He had lovingly drawn me to Him over the years, but this was the first time I looked for God. He specifically and personally showed me something to let me know He was real. From that day, God began to build trust in my heart for Him. Now that I was looking for Him, God knew I'd be ready to see Him in a way that made an impact on my heart.

God is personal. He personally chose you and all the attributes that make you. He wants to show you the love He's always had for you and will forever have for you.

When we really want to know about Who created us, and we look for God, He reveals new insights about Himself that we didn't see, like the artistry in nature that He designed. Have you ever wondered how plants have a set process for stages of growing? The trees have certain groupings. Snow from mountains melts, sending water to lower regions. Rivers lead to other places and often to seas and oceans. These all have nourishing and recycling purposes. Even swarms of fish or birds work together in an undeniable rhythm and unison that defies human understanding.

People call it nature and understand it as scientific discovery. "Look at the science," we hear a lot, but scientists mostly discover something already occurring. They identify the common and orderly elements of pre-existing features. Early scientists actually did know God and wanted to understand what He made. Today, it seems hard for scientists to be amazed by what God created? Even the brilliant minds God gave them are magnificently complex so they can see what's happening down to microscopic levels or light years away. The work of science shows us how enormously complicated humans, creatures and objects of this earth really are. It's taken hundreds of years for us humans to figure out some attributes, but there's always more to discover.

Even medicine is still "practice," with each person's body responding a little differently to everything doctors and researchers try. These are people with God-given minds to be curious with a capacity to comprehend extraordinary levels of intellect focused on trying to understand what they can observe in this world.

Even our beautiful, vast world and the skies above us are abundantly more complicated than they appear. Yet, we are meant to enjoy its beauty and discover the details we're drawn toward knowing.

Nature and medicine are examples, but even in my journey, it wasn't until much later that I appreciated them as true wonders. As a child, we lived at the base of the Rocky Mountains and we went up into them often. In the winter for skiing and the summers for exploring, but I barely paid attention. I enjoyed it, but never thought about it.

Medicine and anatomy were also not a vocation or even a passing interest. Once our son became sick, I wondered more about the disease he has. I wanted to understand what was happening to him, so I learned more about how our bodies work. Awe is an understatement. There are delicate and intricate ways our bodies are designed to work and bring extraordinary balance. Again, it astounds me that doctors who spend dozens of years in college, medical school and training who actively deny God created people. Amoebas are just not that smart. They just cannot gradually become the complicated humans we know we are.

My notice of nature began really when our daughter was young. We would take walks in our neighborhood and she was so curious about everything, especially plants and animals. She loved getting close enough to really enjoy them. Whether dandelions or dogs. There was a persistent curiosity about the natural details of this world. It's so sweet how all children, even once we grow up, are drawn to certain types of discovery or curiosities.

God used her natural curiosity to cause me to wonder, too. At first, I simply was thinking about the answers to her many questions, but then I began to think about it when I was alone. God's beautiful trees give us a soothing calm, especially as we look at a grouping of them. Something about the colors and harmony of it all.

There is also a uniqueness about each tree. Sycamore trees have similar and identifiable traits that other trees do not. A specific sycamore tree has a unique bark pattern or number of branches and leaves. It's orderly with a uniqueness built into each one. From a big picture view, it has a general beauty. Looking closer, it has details that reveal how it's different from the others. This is true even in modified trees and plants. It's also true of people.

God began to help me see His handprint on so many aspects of life that I had just ignored in the busyness of career, parenting, serving, doing, achieving, and the many ways we fill our schedules. Now, I look for Him and the more I do, the more it brings peace. We can turn our minds and focus our eyes to observe the details of nature that we tend to pass as we drive by, jog through, or barely notice from a window. God designed these simply complicated sights long ago and He keeps them for us as reminders that He's involved in our human lives. Have you ever wondered how phenomenally extravagant these "common" parts of nature really are? We often give such a small amount of mental thought to these features, but they can remind us that God has the power to do anything and He's quite creative about it, too.

It's a wonderful journey discovering who God really is. If we begin with what we do know, then we can explore the many amazing insights we don't know. God is abundantly more extraordinary than we can ever imagine. It's been a twenty-plus year journey for me, and every new experience with God captures my heart and brings comfort to my soul. God loves deeply and He desires the same beautiful journey with you.

We're designed to experience the endless love of God who lovingly created you and reveals the many ways He specifically designed you. God loves you personally and as you pursue Him, God will show you it's true.

Love of the Savior

Desperate and Loved
Woman in the Crowd
Matthew 9:20-22; Mark 5:25-34; Luke 8:43-48

"He's coming. They said he just stepped onto the shore. If I get to him, maybe he'll help," the woman whispers to herself.

She moves toward the gathering crowd of people. The town had been talking about this man Jesus doing all sorts of miracles. People rush with hope and curiosity. The woman lifts the cloth of her garment with stains and smells just enough so her feet can move more freely. Others know her, so their eyes growl with disgust or their bodies shift away from possible touch or contact of any kind.

Unclean. Defiled. They believe the woman who bleeds must have sinned in some way for her affliction to remain despite the expense of doctors who tried to resolve it. They assume she did something and few people go near those people.

The woman knows the glances and attitudes of shame. She sees them every day on the streets where she's now penniless and alone. She hears what others say, even when they think she's not listening. Recently, many had been talking about the man named Jesus who's been healing lots of people. Now, He was coming to their town and she had nothing left but an affliction that was getting worse.

She comes near to the sea-like mob around Jesus, then the people shift and press back on her. It absorbs her, forcing her to be within them. She's closer, perhaps close enough.

There's a hush. A desperate man speaking. The woman is barely able to figure out the words. She only hears the man pleading with someone.

"My little daughter is at the point of death. Come and lay your hands on her so that she may be made well and live," the man was asking.

She knows he must be talking to the man Jesus that the townspeople described. She's trying to get a glimpse, but the crowd shifts again, taking her with them.

"Oh, I see Him," she whispers among the people, but speaks only for her benefit. "Yes. It's Him. That's Him. He's not very far now."

She presses her shoulders forward and squeezes toward the man who holds hope for her. Pressing again, she can see Him a few feet away. The human faces and bodies press against each other, desperately trying to be near to the One who heals.

The afflicted woman stretches out her arm with every last ounce of strength she can manage.

"If I touch even His garments, I'll be made well," her thoughts pressing her to try.

As she touches something, it feels like cloth at first but it's strangely responsive.

"What? What?" she whispers as she pulls back her hand quickly.

In her confusion among the throngs of people, her body ebbs and moves involuntarily with the crowd. Something just happened to her. No one sees it. No one feels it, except her. Immediately, she feels the flow of blood dry up. She feels her body is very different.

Then the pressing crowd stands still. The woman stops, unsure of what was happening inside of her and now around her.

The man whose garment she touched stops too. He had felt the power release from His body and He looked around, seeking who had touched Him.

The confused, healed woman instantly becomes terrified.

"What have I done?"

She steps forward and falls down before Jesus. Through tears and trembling she reveals the whole truth of her affliction, poverty, and hope in Him. She cries out that she had reached for Him hoping for even a touch, not worthy of asking or being known. She only had hope. She describes how suddenly the ache, distress, affliction and disappointment vanished. His power had healed her instantly.

She cowers before Him, weeping in fear.

Jesus looks compassionately at the woman. "Daughter, your faith has made you well; go in peace and be healed of your disease."

With those loving words, the tension of her fear releases like an exhaling breath. The One who heals does not bring shame and fear. He brings power that changes us and a love that heals.

As Jesus moves on with the man whose daughter was ill, the crowds go with Him.

The woman remains.

Sitting. Stunned. Amazed.

All these years. All of her money. All of her dignity. All of the people who refused to stay with her. In a moment, the terrible disease that caused it all was gone. She was finally free.

Jesus had healed her, but He had also seen inside her heart. He had the power to heal and the power to know her thoughts. Jesus is the same today. He has the power to heal, and He knows the faith of our hearts. He doesn't walk here in a physical body now because He sits on the throne in heaven. Yet, God didn't leave us alone. The Holy Spirit of God is here now. He works in our hearts and minds today, just as Jesus did.

6

Love . Value . Purpose: Experience God

God is powerful. We've described His divine ability to create the heavens and the earth and have begun to see His power to heal. There's another story God tells about His powerful rescue of His people from the hands of a terrible Pharaoh who harshly enslaved His people for so long. God miraculously pressured Pharaoh to release the people from their slavery. But as they traveled, Pharaoh changed his mind and came to destroy them.

Moses had led the people out of Egypt by God's miraculous hand, but now they were trapped at the edge of the Red Sea with the people panicking. He knew God needed to rescue them again and quickly. Moses stood at the water's edge with his staff and called out to God. With His Divine power, God split the waters which rose up so that bare ground was revealed. All the thousands and possibly millions of God's people went through the waters on dry ground to safety on the other side. The angry pursuers never made it to God's people. God continued to give His people so many more amazing miracles as He worked in their lives and events throughout history. These events are recorded in the Bible and display that God is personal and active. He is also the same today. In someways even more personal and active. This means that we can get to know God more quickly and more personally than at any other time in history.

You may wonder how we can move closer to living in the midst of God's love, value and purpose for us. We can think about God, let our minds wonder about Him, and read the true stories describing Him. It's in the times when we ponder and pursue our Creator that we grow the closest to Him. It's harder if you're distracted, but a treasure when you do let yourself pursue God. Try to find time to sit with the One who declares He has great love for you. Just as you desire for Him to pay attention to you, He loves when you come to spend time with Him.

One way we can shift our thinking is to remember God loves every person and displays His love through creation and rescue. God has individual and personal ways He made you and thought about you. He knew long ago that you would fit perfectly into this moment of time. He's loving to all and also loves you.

God loves us in many ways, but we can describe two of them here. One is generally as people and the second is in a personal individual way. Look at people. He made humans generally the same in the sense that we are not dolphins or caterpillars. We're also very specifically unique. He loves generally and personally. That's why a general love for God is not enough to fill us. We're designed by God for more than a general belief or distant love for Him. To experience the personal love of God, we have to look more closely. Looking from a distance helps us with one side of identifying God. Just like you, it's in the specific personal ways you exist that make you who you are. To believe and know the personal love of God, we can get a closer look at Him and begin to ask about Him. And it's really worth our time.

God wants to give you wonderful insights and discoveries about who He is. One of my favorite understandings about God is in this verse.

> *"The Lord who made the earth, the Lord who formed it to establish it — the Lord is His name: call to Me and I will answer you and I will tell you great and hidden things that you have not known."*
> — Jeremiah 33:2-3

God put this in the Bible originally talking to the Israelites, but He also tells us later in the Bible that He will give His wisdom generously (James 1:5) and His Spirit will lead us into all truth (John 16:13). We just have to believe that He will.

God, the Creator of magnificently beautiful wonders of the earth and wonders inside of you wants to tell you hidden revelations and wisdom for your life!

God does not want you to follow a bunch of rules to know who He is. That's a misguided attitude for God and removes the love and kindness of God's heart. God wants you to spend time with Him. That's a personal attitude toward God. Since He created so many extraordinary things, we can imagine and ask God what He wants to show us about those things.

Spending time with God can change your life in great and unexpected ways. Perhaps you're not sure how to do that. It's all about your heart attitude for God. It's about you personally wanting to spend time with Him.

Loving God and His love for us is God's main theme throughout all of the Bible because it's who He is. Powerful and personal.

Our time with God shouldn't be about the pressure of performing or doing all the right things. It can be as simple as talking to God and asking Him to show you something new. This can bring calm to a bad day or stressful time. On the hard days especially, it can help to remember God's bigness and powerful greatness. It can help us to realize He sees everything that weighs on us, but He's also big enough to handle it for us. God loves us always and spending time with Him brings the power of His pure love and peace to rest upon us to calm our hearts.

Since some may not know where to start with God, this little acronym may help guide you as a way to pursue Him.

OPEN your heart and mind to God. Discover wonderful ways and truths about His love, value and purposes in your life.

O.P.E.N.

Offer. Praise. Explore. New Perspective.

O . . . Offer. Begin by offering your heart and mind to God in a quiet place. It helps our minds focus on wanting to know what God's love for us looks like. We just simply let Him know we want to be with Him. This gives us a moment to transition to being with God in a personal way. You could simply say, "God, I'm here and I want to spend time with you."

P . . . Praise. This connects our hearts to the reality that God is God, and He loves you. Celebrate His goodness, love, peace, healing and presence that He promises. He is the Creator of the heavens and the earth who spoke and then it existed. This is our great God, and He loves you. We're praising Him because of how great He is and how He loves us personally. We praise God that He wants to show us more of Himself.

E . . . Explore. God knows all the ways that will touch your heart. We can ask God to show us what He wants us to know. This is about exploring and experiencing God. It can be places in the Bible or topics where our hearts need healing or redeeming.

(**N** is coming in a minute...)

At first, it can be hard to wait to see what God might show you. It's hard to be still because we're so used to being busy. You could write in a journal or just sit there with your Bible. Perhaps you'll hear or think of a word or topic.

Go to that place in the Bible. There's usually a subject list in the back or you can search an online Bible for that word.

Then ask the Lord, "God what do You want to show me? You know every part of me. I want to know You better. Please show me so that I can understand."

If a certain idea isn't coming to mind, I suggest trying these few options. The Bible is organized by "books." Try the "books" of Luke, John, or the Psalms. It helps to read Luke or John from their beginning and discover the unfolding story of Jesus during His short thirty-some years walking on earth. Luke was a physician and traveled with many of those who knew Jesus. John was very close with Jesus and he describes his experience with Him. Some of the stories overlap, but each writer highlights certain details more than others. (This is part of a group of "books" called the "Gospels." I'll describe them a little later.)

In Psalms, many "chapters" or "psalms" were recorded by King David. He was a shepherd, musician, warrior and filled with intense love for God. God made him the king over God's people in Israel and Judah. David would cry out to God in his anguish, but also in his joy. King David always knew deeply in his heart that God is mighty and merciful, and that God is big enough to hear his sorrow and fear, but also able to rescue him from it.

These are ways we can explore truths about God and begin to "hear" about His compassion and rescue. When you're not sure what something means or how it relates to you, keep asking God. Sometimes something will happen in your day or someone will say something that exactly reminds you of what you read. God is not limited and often

He will you show you He's paying attention to you in unexpected ways. Hold these moments and take this goodness into your heart.

There will also be those times when you'll read words in the Bible and it feels like they were written just for you and for that moment. Treasure these beautiful moments from God as well. He's revealing Himself to you personally, not just generally.

N ... New Perspective. God will give you a new perspective. Sometimes we're confused about circumstances we're experiencing, or we miss what He knows is happening. Often, we've let the outside influences guide our inside thoughts and attitudes. God is different. He sees you from the inside and with His great love and value. He sees His design for you and how it brings freedom and understanding. These are ways He uniquely chose you for this world. Whether it's your laughter, wisdom, creativity, perseverance or millions of other possibilities. God placed those wonderful features within you, and He enjoys exploring His vision for you and with you.

As He begins to reveal those beautiful parts of you and the truths of who He is, a new perspective will emerge for you. This experience begins to create a greater love for God and a longing to know more of those previously unknown ideas and thoughts He enjoys sharing with you personally.

New and wonderful understandings begin to appear, and you start to see yourself and the world differently. As you fill up with His love and His value for you and for others, you will see evidence of His transforming love in your thoughts and your days. You'll begin to overflow with love for Him, embracing His love for you and wanting to share that love with others.

Opening our hearts to God gives us the experience of being with God. These personal experiences bring in God's healing and hope-filled presence into the crevices of your soul that need His goodness.

Love of the Savior

Love. Sacrifice. Provision.
Jesus Feeds 5000
Matthew 14:13-21; Mark 6:30-43;
Luke 9:10-17; John 6:1-14

The sun was setting and those healed by Jesus still lingered in the crowd. For so many, the great Man with compassion was hard to leave and they wanted to be near Him. To stay longer.

In the crowd, the little boy looks up at his mother. "When can we go home? Will we eat soon?" he says with childhood curiosity.

For his mother, the amazing experience of the day was beginning to bring a touch of exhaustion. She looks at her son, then toward the Man with compassion and miraculous powers who had healed thousands among them. As she watches the Man speak to the ones who are with Him, she can hear them say something about not having enough for everyone to eat.

Looking into her son's eager eyes as he waits for his mother's response, she struggles with her thoughts. "Should we leave? Return home? But what about those helping Jesus? They're hungry too." She has loaves of bread and some fish for the long journey. She reaches in her bag for the food.

She kneels before her son. She holds the food before him and speaks directly to the boy.

"Take all of these to Jesus, who healed so many people today. He will give us food."

"Mama, I don't understand. Isn't this food?"

"It is my son, but many more are hungry. Jesus will make sure it is enough."

"Okay, Mama," the boy replies without wondering if his mother was mistaken.

She watches the boy weave through the few groups of people until he walks up behind one of the men. He tugs on the man's clothing.

"Excuse me," the boy says in a matter-of-fact delivery tone. "My mama says to give you this food. That Jesus would make it enough for everyone."

Jesus smiles as He watches the disciple respond with surprise to the boy. The child hands over the food and stands straight, showing his responsible, grown-up look. He had completed the task Mama gave him.

The boy's mother watches with peaceful pleasure rising up within her. She sees the eyes of Jesus as He too watches the boy return to her. His eyes have a knowingness of her sacrifice. She's not sure how Jesus knows. It's the way He looks at her son and catches her gaze. She knows He will feed the hungry people. The mother feels a deep, overwhelming thankfulness for her day and all she's witnessed.

So many lives changed and bodies healed.

The boy wraps his arms around his mother, "Like you said, Mama. I gave them the food. Will we eat now?" he says with the same curiosity of his earlier questions.

Her eyes linger toward Jesus a touch longer and her heart pulses with joy.

Jesus. The Healer.

She tucks her son in closer and kisses his head. She turns back to watch Jesus. He raises His head as well as the bread toward heaven with blessings. Then, the people begin to sit in large groups. Jesus and the men give food to every family. The food never decreases in all the baskets as the men walk around to everyone.

The boy and his family eat well. The woman looks around, smiles and notices that everyone had plenty to eat. She also sees something as they sit resting after the meal. There are many baskets still full of food. She begins counting . . . 12 baskets, full of food.

The blessings and miracles of this day seemed endless to the woman. But now, seeing the added increase beyond what was needed gives her greater joy. God didn't need to make the extra, but He did. The abundant goodness makes her chuckle just a bit because it was like her day, precious beyond expected. She would always remember God's abundant goodness. May we also remember to ask God for His abundant goodness in our lives as well.

Love of the Savior

Healing Love of Jesus
Jesus Heals Boy with Unclean Spirit
Matthew 17:14-20; Mark 9:14-29; Luke 9:37-43

The woman was kneading the dough. Thunk, press, turn. Thunk, press, turn. The practiced rhythm of her bread making is a background for her motherly ears listening to the nearby children. They are not her own, but her sister's children. Yet, she knows to listen for trouble. Instinctively waiting for sudden shifts in voices or sounds alerting her to a need for intervention.

Then, she hears the sound of hooves approaching and a faint voice.

"Mother, Mother," she hears and knows it's her husband's voice. Her heart jumps and its pace accelerates. She drops her dough and wipes her hands while she scurries to the entrance. Her feet are swift, and her mind is racing.

"They return! Sister, my husband and son!" she calls out to her family.

Her heart fills with fear and hope. Her vision is hazy with tears. Rushing out the doorway, her footsteps quicken. Her husband walks alongside their donkey with their son sitting on top.

"Oh husband, you return!" she cries out, but her eyes are not fully on him.

Her eyes are on the boy. She's watching for him to fall, to be thrown down again. Her thoughts flash back to the aching moments of her son thrashing on the ground, and as if at the hands of something unseen, then thrown into fire and deep waters. As the two come closer, her steps bring her right to them and her husband slows the donkey.

The boy cries out to his mother, "Mama, I'm all okay now. The man Jesus healed me."

The woman covers her mouth in shock, catching her sound of surprise. The beginning tears are overflowing now.

"What, dear son? What did you say? Husband is this true? Tell me," she urges and waits. Her body trembles and her heart overwhelmed. She falls into the arms of her husband.

"Oh, dear wife, do not weep," he says to her. He holds her in his arms, feeling the exhaustion of her mother's heart and tears of a mother's sorrow. "Dear mother, he is well now. He is free now," he speaks gently to her, embracing her. "Mother, look at your son."

The father releases the woman so he can help the child from the donkey. The boy leans into his father's up-stretched hands and arms. The strength of his arms guiding the boy safely to stand on the ground.

The boy stands up as tall as he can and faces his mother.

"Mama, I don't have those evil things in me anymore. They can't hurt me anymore," his sweet, young voice rejoices.

Kneeling to the ground, she pulls the boy into her arms and weeps with deep joy. Her body fills with a thankfulness she doesn't know how to manage. There had been days and days and days of watching her son thrash around and foaming at the mouth uncontrollably. They couldn't stop him. The many ways she and her husband tried to hold him, but the violent movements ripped him away from them.

As she holds her son now, his body is calm and peaceful. Stroking his head and kissing the side of his face, she can feel the reality of joy rising up within her. The sorrow and ache for her son was being pressed out of her. Joy and peace began to fill her soul.

She stands, leaving one arm on her son's shoulders and asks her husband, "Tell me everything. What happened? Please. Let me know how our boy is healed."

The father puts his arm around her shoulders with one hand and guides them forward. As they walk toward the house where his relatives, nieces and nephews wait for them, he begins to tell of their miraculous experience with Jesus.

The mother feels comforted by your husband's arms and the body of her son next to her. She eagerly holds onto every word. They'd heard about Jesus and hoped He could help them. After all the many years of sorrow, their desperate prayers to the Lord had been answered.

"We went to the Sea of Galilee, just as our family told us. We went along the shore and its towns, listening for what the people might tell us about Jesus of Nazareth. We came to a town where the people said that disciples following Jesus had come and they also could heal."

"How could they heal also? Did they heal our son? I don't understand," she asks.

"These men told the people about the kingdom of God and that Jesus had given them authority to heal."

"But you said Jesus healed our son? No?"

"Patience, my love. Many parts to this story," he says as he pats her shoulder with a gentle squeeze. "We found the men from Jesus and watched them send demons fleeing from people and cured diseases. They always spoke of Jesus and His kingdom. So, the boy and I came to them. They heard all that I had to say about how horrible episodes happened to our son. They earnestly tried to do for us what they had done for many others, but nothing. Oh, my heart was so very sad. The scribes were arguing, and others were arguing about why they couldn't heal our son.

"Then four men were coming down from the mountain. The disciples looked up and saw Him. They told us Jesus was with those men. He would help our son."

"What was He like? This man Jesus, what was He like?" the mother interrupts.

"He was someone like I've never seen. He was a man, but something just emanated from Him. Just as our relatives said. It's as if the presence of God walks within Him. I was mesmerized by Him and I couldn't wait for the disciples to take me to Him. I'm embarrassed to say, dear wife, but my love for our son just burst out and I cried out to Jesus. I called, 'Teacher, I beg you to look at my son, for he is my only child. Please, a spirit seizes him, and he cries out suddenly. It convulses him. He foams at the mouth. It shatters him and will hardly leave.'"

Love ~ Value ~ Purpose

The woman tucks her head in closer, smiling at the thought of him yelling it out.

Continuing, the father says, "Then as the Teacher came near, I was trembling. He was kind in His eyes. He came right up to me and asked questions. I told Him that His disciples could not heal our son. The Lord spoke of how many people had much unbelief."

"What happened then?"

"I cried out to Him, 'Help my unbelief!' Oh, dear wife, I was overwhelmed."

Treasuring every detail, she encourages him to keep going, "Dear husband, you love your son. You're such a good man. Oh, thank you for taking our son to be saved."

"Dear wife, the majesty of God came upon that place. Even as our son came near Jesus, the evil tried to hurt him more. It threw him to the ground again, but Jesus didn't move away. He was not afraid at all. He rebuked the evil that hurt our son, but then our boy lay there completely still. The people thought he was dead."

"Was he dead? Oh goodness. I wanted to be there with you and longed to be there with you. Now, I know that my heart would not have survived," she interjects.

"Dear one, it is well. I know the Lord held me still even though everyone was so quiet. Then, Jesus took our son by the hand and the boy arose. Oh, what joy!" he exclaimed, recalling the moment.

"Oh husband, just that quickly?" she said with genuine shock. "Just lifted him by the hand?"

Then a sweet voice spoke, "Yes, Mama. He touched my hand and I felt like I was being put up standing. I wasn't standing up by myself. I was just suddenly standing. And I was okay, Mama. I felt all the bad inside of me was all the way gone!" he declared with his childlike excitement.

The parents of the boy stop. They both kneel to see him at eye level. The three embrace each other and praise God. As they rejoice, the family near the doorway leaves their careful watching position and begin to praise God for His majesty too. The families rejoice that Jesus had healed the innocent, sweet boy they loved.

Love ~ Value ~ Purpose

7

Value: Outside Influence

There are lots of ways life gets complicated and we get off track from God's loving perspective about who we are and how we can see the world. The main obstacles are things that happen outside of us and how we understand and translate it on the inside. We get jumbled up inside because we're taught to look at ourselves in reverse. We've learned to look at the events and people around us to decide what and who we are. For this chapter, let's look at how the outside impacts our inside. Then in the next chapter, we'll look at how God can reset that for us.

We have impressions of how humans do life and how we understand bad elements in the world. There are basic ways we are influenced from outside. First, people communicate to us in various ways. This is done in a general way for society and personally in our interactions. Second, Satan seeks to distract and harm us generally and personally as well.

Various types of information can get to us from external places, but only you and God are the ones who can truly know what's happening on the inside of you. Often, these outside elements influence us more than we realize. It's not always easy to know how much and which ones are causing harm. There are the obvious ones, but then there are sneakier ones.

Let's start with communication and people. We've described that God loves generally and personally. God values everyone generally, but also specifically. God interacts with us generally as humans, but personally when we're willing. So, it makes sense that people relate to one another in general societal ways as well as personal ways. We absorb information generally from the voices speaking through various electronic means and the images magnified, praised, or distributed. Society and those who communicate with the world have thoughts, attitudes and ideas they desire to share. This can be good, bad, helpful, degrading, inspiring, or ignored. Its impact can be as large as the number of words we can assign to them. As individuals in society, we receive this communication from other people in a general way and often.

Communication can be personal as well. You talk to your friends and family. You join groups or churches. Even with COVID-19, we've found ways to communicate with other individuals in personal ways. We grow up learning to communicate and to live our lives practicing how we interact with each other almost every day. We relate to each oth-

Value: Outside Influence

er as individuals to individuals. Sometimes we're in groups and other times not. This is not meant to oversimplify, but to give us a general concept to recognize.

Communication comes from the outside and it can go into your heart, mind and soul. These come from all different sources. It can be good and bad. The challenge is that there's so much bad these days and it's an enormous volume. Lately, it seems we don't find good as much as we see shades of bad. Again, the extreme bad is easier to see, but even a focus on good can get twisted to bad. Like serving others.

We often serve because others like seeing us do good activities. We don't do this on purpose. We're encouraged to do noble works. This starts off well, biblically actually. God says to love the Lord your God with all your heart, mind, and soul and love others as yourself. But often we serve because we are expected to do good for society. It's not bad to want people to do and show kindness for others. What we're trying to practice here is seeing what's going on in our hearts and *why* we do things.

Sometimes people end up praising the *doing* part and not the loving part. It can become *doing* good for God and *doing* things for others. Goodness *is* good. *Doing* to show others your goodness is *not*.

God truly loves those we help more than we do and before we do. True loving happens when we remember *why* we help. God deeply loves that person, and they are in need. God desires for every person to know His love and you may be the person who reveals His true love for them. When our hearts are so thankful for God's love for us, we'll want to share His goodness through us. It's about letting God love them through us. This genuine love brings an abundance of authentic joy. It is precisely because God knows the needs of people that our attitude toward them is important to Him.

Doing out of obligation or to get a feel-good glance from our peers removes the love God wants to reveal to that real person who desires and needs authentic, pure love, just as God has been revealing to you.

It is deeply different. But wait. Don't cancel all the good you're doing. The key is to love as God loves and sees others as He sees them. As you do, ask God to shape your heart and thoughts to share His love with someone and to treasure experiencing it with Him. Seeing God first and His heart for you and every person shifts our reason for bringing care to others in great need. Our heart attitude matters to God. He loves every single person in need abundantly more than we do and He wants them to experience genuine care and genuine love, not expedient doing out of obligation.

When we find ourselves shifting our behaviors to do what others want rather than what God may be asking of us, we're letting this outside communication change our focus. It begins to alter how we view ourselves. We take in all this communication and it changes how we see ourselves. We can wonder what the reactions and behaviors of others say about us. They like it when we do activities and show interest, so we may want to do more because their responses feel good to us, rewarding almost. Unfortunately, we're trained to be heavily influenced by this communication.

Remember, our heart attitude is important to God because it's a filter for how we view everything else. Our heart filters function best when we see our experiences through the eyes of God's love and value for us and others. Helping others is deeply meaningful to God, but why we help others also has an effect on us. Your heart is the most important part of you. It connects you personally and deeply with God. What overflows out of our hearts is how we can authentically share His love for each person God puts in our path or urges us to pursue in care.

Then, there's another significant outside influence.

> *"Your enemy the devil prowls around like a roaring lion looking for someone to devour."*
> — 1 Peter 5:8, NIV

Let's look at ways evil thoughts and events try to influence you, too.

It doesn't take much effort to think about heart wounds in your life or to see the destruction around us. We see it when people hurt others with their words, attitudes, or actions. What the Bible reveals to us is that some angels wanted to be God. Since that wasn't possible, God sent them away from Him. Not liking this banishment, their pride turned into hatred and anger. These angelic beings make it their purpose to cause you harm and pull you away from the true healing and peaceful love of God who created you. The most effective way this is done is to distract us, hurt us, or present a mirage of goodness leading to a place of misery for our hearts. It piles on us, then our children, then their children. It happens in every culture, but in America, we tend to be drawn to high-ranking jobs, money or numbers of "friends" and "followers." We like to pile up the evidence of how valuable we are to society. These bad beings use these outside influences of the world to bring harm right to you. It does this personally and through society. We don't often notice it, but we often fall for it.

Now let's look at how God combats the reality of the devil trying to cause you harm through that same Bible passage.

> *"Cast all your anxiety on Him [God] because He cares for you. Be alert and of sober mind.* Your enemy the devil prowls around like a roaring lion looking for someone to devour. *Resist him, standing firm in the faith."*
> — 1 Peter 5:7-9 (NIV, emphasis added)

Notice how God uses these words to block the devil on either side. We can turn to God because He cares about us. We can practice being aware of what we see or hear. When it doesn't feel right or it's clearly bad, we say, "No. I choose God." You can tell God how you're hurt, bothered or confused by what happened or what you saw. If you're looking at God and telling the devil, "No," then evil can't get your full attention. By resisting the ploys of the devil, we stop more of his harm from getting inside of us.

In another part of the Bible, God says, "Submit to yourselves, therefore to God. Resist the devil and he will flee from you" (James 4:7). This is the same idea. Choose God because He loves you. Remember, Satan wants to devour you.

God is your rescuer. God loves you. God created you. God shows us how He protects us from the harshness of the enemy trying to hurt us. We call to Him for rescue. We don't exactly have to go to "war" with evil, and we don't need to be afraid of it either.

We simply say, "No. I believe God loves me and devil you want to devour me. I choose God."

We can do this when the devil tries to push his harm through images we see in society or a distraction into our lives and thoughts. When he causes harm somewhere in the world and we watch the video. It influences us, but we can do something. We can praise God that He sees Satan's evil harm and we ask God to stop the evil in its tracks. Ask God to stop it from destroying the people and the lives that we're seeing in the images. "God, please be with these people. Please stop the evil and bring peace."

Personally, when we hear or see images that make us feel bad about someone else or ourselves, we can do the same thing. "God, you love me. You created me. Please rescue me. I reject these words and images that hurt me. I choose you because You love me."

Another area to be watchful is busyness. Sometimes being really busy doing lots of productive or useful projects can be a tricky way evil tries to distract us. When we feel overstretched or over-tired, it's important to sit with God. Ask Him to show you what He wants you to do and to help you see which activities are best for you.

Finally, one of the most difficult outside influences are those deeply, hurtful wounds to your heart, mind or body. Evil wants people to inflict harm on us, then he tries to keep the damage inside of you to increase the effects of it all. This twisted evil is a lie Satan often uses.

When someone hurts us badly, there can be shock, pain and confusion from what happened. Satan enjoys this and he tries to make it worse. He causes us to relive it over and over. The initial wrong becomes an ongoing opportunity for damage to replay in our minds. This drives the pain deeper and creates a toxic bitterness and resentment. The short answer is that forgiveness is God's unexpected and extraordinary victory to push away this toxic weapon of Satan. It's also one of the hardest to understand and embrace without the love and revelation of God showing you why. For now, please know that we can be freed from the lie of revenge, or even just vengeful grudges. I don't want to belittle any damage done to you, for I have been damaged myself. This is why God had me include a chapter that addresses it more (Chapter 9). Please know God sees your injury and we will address it more fully.

For now, you may be thinking, "She has no idea what I've been through," or "But what do I do with the evil that's happening to me every day?" It's true. I don't know your story. God does and He wants to heal, rescue, revive, and infuse hope and restoration to all of your wounds. For me, I do know physical wounds. I do know ongoing emotional wounds. I do know neglect. I also know the impact of those wounds. I know my response of "over-achieving" and doing everything in the right way, for the right people, to get the right response. I know trying to figure out why I'm here by gaining praise through accomplishments. I know the deep ache of watching our child suffer medically and others we love struggle or pass away. I know the deep hope and waiting in all my prayers for miracles and simple daily needs.

My challenges are not as difficult as many, yet harder than some as well. I used to think I would have picked the trials differently, but then I would've missed so much of God's heart. I do believe that if I had run into the loving arms of God sooner, the trials would not have lasted as long. During our difficult times, God can show us intense love and encouragement. God's wonderful love and peace can soothe and transform your heart. You can know He loves you and can be healed by that love.

The experiences of our life can draw us to God. His kindness can give us the willingness to be vulnerable with Him, to ask "why," but also, "can you help me understand what's going on?" He helps to reset personal relationships by shaping them toward His heart for us. It becomes less focused on a self-drive to fix or to make everything the way we think is best, and more of seeing yourself and others through God's heart of love and value.

Toward healing, God will delicately bring forward memories that cause pain, but only so He can heal them, remove the impact, and replace the pain with peace. Even ongoing broken relationships can begin to shift as He deepens His imprint of love, value and purpose into your heart, mind and soul.

Sadly, the toxic ways of this world mislead us and cause harm. Its distraction is being absorbed deeply into our hearts and minds. But our days can change, and we can experience life in a whole new way. Whether it's really hard details of life or just unexpected matters that suddenly show up in your day. As humans, we just can't fix it, but we try. God gives new eyes and new hearts to push out the toxic influence and lets us welcome in His goodness. This effort to press out the toxic bad and welcome in pure love, joy, and peace is our path to becoming whole.

This is why knowing God matters so much. He's the only one who can free us and fill us well. God created the wonders of the heavens and the earth. God did that for people, and He also did that for you. The abundances of this earth are not just random objects that He dropped onto it. He lovingly and purposefully chose to make it for all of us and each of us. Then, He designed every person with many intricate details that science is only beginning to discover. He placed each one carefully into a time in history to interact with certain other individuals He created. God chose this all to reveal the ways He cares about every person in a personal way.

You are part of that creation. You matter to God and He loves you. He knows what ignites your heart with joy because He put that inside of you. He also knows the most intricate ways you've been injured, and sometimes it's more than you let yourself realize. Who is better qualified to help than the One who miraculously designed you?

Love of the Savior

You Matter
Woman in Synagogue on the Sabbath
Luke 13:10-17

The aches in her back travel down her legs and to her feet. She clings to the wooden cane that holds her from falling. Her back curls forward so she has to tilt her head a bit to the side to see ahead. The woman carefully sits down near the back of the synagogue. The place she devotedly comes to worship the Lord. This day, a man is speaking and teaching. The people listen as he talks about the kingdom of God.

His words are comforting to her somehow, even with the constant pain of her body.

"He is kind," she thinks to herself.

She watches his arms, head and eyes as the man speaks with such great authority. The words are wise, but she still understands them in her simple ways.

"There's something in this man, Lord, what is it?" she ponders silently, praying in this holy place she loves.

As the man is teaching in the synagogue, He looks her way and pauses. He sees her. She feels Him see her. There's a flutter in her stomach and something causes her heart to quicken. His eyes are on her, then He motions to her and calls her over to Him.

The leaders of the synagogue twist their bodies and heads to see the person He's calling. They have stern looks on their faces as she carefully tries to stand, never being able to stand up fully.

A quiet hum fills the synagogue as the people watch the woman who cannot stand up, but crouches as she walks. She's on display for all of them to view as she inches her way forward.

She presses her body ahead as she passes the many eyes of those waiting for her. Over these last eighteen years, she's adjusted her thoughts to expect the gaze, so their stares don't detract her. She's drawn to the Teacher before her. The kind and sure way He spoke of God's kingdom. His eyes have patience in them as she awkwardly shifts and walks the many steps to Him.

She's near Him now and He steps right in front of her crippled body. She tries to look all the way up to His eyes and refocus on Him, but she can't quite see His face now.

Then she hears His voice again, "You are freed from your disability," He says.

At His words, she responds without thinking and takes in a sudden gasp of air. She feels her body pulsing. The cry of her heart that ached for eighteen years now struggles to match the sudden swirling thoughts of her mind.

"Freed from my disability…what's He saying…how is He saying…O Lord God let it be," she whimpers in her heart and mind without a word leaving her lips.

Then, He places His hand with a gentle touch upon her feeble body and curled-over back. It feels like a soothing warm brook of cleansing water is trickling from His hand into her body. The traveling warmth quickly runs through her body and she blinks her eyes. Then her back lifts, slowly at first, then smoothly. She stands straight up and lifts her head the way others in the synagogue would do with ease. Her eyes rise up to the One who had called her to come forward. The One who touched her back and freed her from her infirmities.

Now, she can easily look into the loving eyes of the Lord who had freed her. Without pause or care for the room filled with people behind her, she praises Him.

"Oh Lord, glory and honor and praise to you!"

She raises her hands high and praises the Lord for healing her of the disabling spirit that harmed her every day for eighteen years. Rejoicing and praising Him.

Jesus smiles and receives the joy and praise from the once feeble woman.

But as she rejoices, the elders of the synagogue shift in their places, with stern mouths and faces. They stand, indignant. The ruler of the synagogue turns to the people. With a raised voice over the stirring of rejoicing in the room, the ruler says, "There are six days in which work ought to be done. Come on those days and be healed, and not on the Sabbath day!"

The crowd quiets, confused by the declaration of their leader. The heads turn back and forth to one another, wondering what to think. The Sabbath is for rest and honoring the Lord. No work on the Sabbath. The confusion quenches the rejoicing. There's a pause in the room.

Eyes and attention shift to Jesus, who had healed the woman of a disabling spirit that once harmed her. Jesus looks directly at the ruler of the synagogue.

The priest who claimed authority of the ways of God made his physical stance taller, strengthening his commitment to the declaration.

Jesus responds with a firm assurance, "You hypocrites. Does not each of you on the Sabbath untie his ox or his donkey from the manger and lead it away to water it? And ought not this woman, a daughter of Abraham, whom Satan bound for eighteen years, be loosed from this bond on the Sabbath day?"

The woman stands up straight next to Jesus. She loved the Lord and what He had done for her. Now, she doesn't know what to do. After Jesus spoke those words, she turns to look at those who guide this synagogue and God's people in this holy place.

She silently and nervously wonders, "Would they deny the goodness and blessing that Jesus gave me?"

The woman knows Jesus had been telling them all of the kingdom of God with such wisdom and authority. Then, He used that authority to heal. How would they respond to this healing of a daughter of Abraham? Even in her confusion, her overflowing joy could not be muffled any longer. It's not to be quenched by their reactions to Jesus healing her. He had done something they had not done for her in all these years. She knows God healed her.

Slowly, these men close their eyes, drop their heads, then curl their shoulders in shame. Their bodies reveal what was happening in their hearts. They know it's not work to heal on the Sabbath. It's not work to give hope and life on the Sabbath. For what better way to bring rest and honor to the Lord Almighty than to receive it with joy and to praise Him for it.

The mood of confusion shifts. All the people in the synagogue begin again to rejoice and praise the Lord for all the glorious wonders He had done.

And the woman who once walked bent over, with an awkward tilt of her head to see before her, now walks upright and rejoices with all the people. This was the day the Lord Jesus touched and healed her body and captured her heart.

8

Value: Inside Reset

God loves and values everyone. We don't acquire or earn it from other people. Not understanding this turns our thinking in the reverse direction. The world would have us define love, value and purpose through their eyes. God's eyesight is so much better. To reset our thinking, we can begin to rely on God's thoughts about us to guide who we are instead of the world's ideas leading us somewhere else.

God's wisdom and love are the most effective way to reset from generations of reverse thinking or simply the barrage of pressure through all things electronic. This is why He draws us to Him with the grandeur of His creation and seeing goodness in the little moments. It's God's invitation for you to discover a peaceful place inside that He knows you'll love.

The more you experience and learn about God's love and protection, the easier it is to see what's against that goodness. The Bible is really the best place to prepare you for spotting a fake. Here's why. As you read what it really says, you begin to "hear" and "see" how God thinks. When you hear and see Him in this way, you begin to recognize His love and heart for you in a deeper way. This helps us to more quickly recognize when something is not as it appears. We don't need to live in a cave or remove ourselves from this world, but we do need to know how to get true information.

For those not familiar with the Bible, this is a very basic rundown of how it's laid out. First, God wanted us to know who He is and how He thinks, so He recorded it. This is the Bible. His words for us are so that we don't have to feel alone or misunderstand who He is. The "Old Testament" describes God's story of creating the world and how humans messed up by believing a lie. Yet, God still builds up His people with His power and presence with them, then He gives hints about what's coming.

Next, the "New Testament" begins with Jesus coming down from Heaven to walk among humanity, healing the bodies and minds of many. Adam and Eve messed up and this caused the rest of us to live with it, so Jesus gave His life for everyone's sin as the way to fix it. This is covered in four "books" called "Gospels," which means good news. These are titled, "Matthew," "Mark," "Luke," and "John." The remaining part of the Bible records about 100 years of what early believers saw or learned about what Jesus did and how they experienced their faith in Him. Most of these individuals began their journey in the Jewish faith as a continuation of God's people from the "Old Testament" times, but then God wanted more people outside this group to be close to Him too.

This is where our understanding of God loving everyone is important. God transitioned the history of the world to more than declaring His love for every person. He began to be with us personally. God does this by placing His Spirit into all who believe in Jesus.

It's not the same system from early history, but the same heart of God coming in a greater way. Now all of us can be closer to God, not just certain people chosen to speak personally with God. These are not separate stories. God progressively reveals Himself to the people He created. Humans experienced wounded hearts throughout all of history. With Jesus, God gave the world a way to be free from so much of it, but also a promise to spend forever with Him.

In the "Old Testament," there is so much humanity in the pages. The people love God, forget about Him and they're drawn to the society and cultures around them. This leads to doing evil to others and corrupting the pure thoughts and behaviors honoring God. They begin to face misery from all the bad choices, then they cry out to God to help them and yearn for Him in their hearts. When they realize they've forgotten what protects them, they turn their hearts back to God. They know their misery can only be relieved by the God who created them, loves them, and brought them strength and peace.

This cycle repeated often in history. It still repeats today. Long ago, people were influenced by elements outside of themselves and God. The same is true today.

In the "New Testament," we see the compassion and power of Jesus, then the Holy Spirit. We discover a new way to step outside that human cycle. The core truths are still there: God loves and values us. He blesses us. The human cycle is also still there. We appreciate it, then continue on with our lives. We get distracted and gradually don't notice God or decide He's irrelevant and far away. God becomes no longer personal to us, but a general thought. Until life and pressure gets personal and begins to hurt or press in on us.

We often apply mental reasoning to our situation for a while. Some blame God and others try to fix it on their own. Others give up and check out. But some do what many people in history did. Cry out to God because no human can fix what's destroying them.

God's people had a cycle. We have a cycle. God wants to free us from the destructive cycles. Our inside is designed by God but gets sidetracked by sin — ours, others and some attempts by evil beings. The outside things impact us on the inside when we let it. God breaks it by resetting us on the inside. For those who let God break the cycle, they don't have to keep letting in all the harmful stuff anymore. Through the Holy Spirit, we can see moments and experiences more clearly and stop pesky thoughts before they drag us into destructive cycles.

Inside is where our emotional, spiritual, and intellectual treasure is, so it makes a difference when you know God loves you and created you with His precious imprint. He loves spending time with you and sees all the value He put in you. To heal the broken parts and wounds, God works from inside through His Spirit. This is what protects us from the human cycle.

You matter to Him. We're designed to get our joy, peace, strength, wisdom, and provision from God. God decided who you are. God loves you and you need His love to protect you from what people say and do to you. The more we embrace and live our lives as God sees us and through

His loving heart, the easier it is to guard ourselves from the devouring attempts coming from outside of us.

You have an image of yourself. You likely chose this through a collection of people's ideas and images you've seen. We talked about the influences outside of you as people, communication, and Satan sprinkling harmful ideas at various times in your life from his viewpoint. This external collection can define you over time — for good or bad. These outside things shape your thoughts and attitudes, but also how you see yourself.

God has the master plan for you, with all the intricate personal details that make you precious. The world around you was not there when God put your design together and it doesn't know all the details. Sure, they can know generally about you, even some quite personally. They don't know everything and haven't seen all of your days. God has plans for you that only you can share with this world. God made you and wanted you to be the one to discover what others cannot know about you from the heart of God. He wants His pure love, joy, and peace to fill you and reveal precious discoveries to you.

Embracing God for who He is and how much He loves you brings a new truth to our concept of value. Being loved and valued by God changes how we experience this human world. Your value is important to God. It's important for why He placed you here at this time in history, and how you can share that with others.

Your value begins with the Creator's love for you. We struggle with knowing what love is because humanity didn't create it. We struggle to define value when we look anywhere else but God. A collection of ideas, thoughts, and attitudes about love and value from other sources will change. With more and more of us looking to these constantly shifting resources to define love and value, it eventually crumbles. It cannot bear the weight of millions of people dangling their thoughts and hoping it might work.

God is the only One big enough to sort it all out for you. Do you want to sort through millions of ideas collected into shifting chaos? Or do you want to hear from the One who spoke, and this extraordinarily complicated world came into existence? God knows how to understand complicated things. God thought about all the amazing ways He wanted to make you, then He created you. Remember, the Creator loves every person He makes. There's nothing on this earth that can understand value and worth like God does. He creates value and you are His precious one of great value.

As we open our hearts, minds, and eyes to God in our days, we can begin to know these truths are real. As we feel and recognize God's true love and value, we can see how our reverse thinking is turning around. Similar to our discussion of how to OPEN our hearts to God, the more we pursue Him the more we recognize He's making the changes — we aren't doing the hard work. God is. When we spend time to sit and look to Him, then He changes us. We get to discover what He's done!

Knowing these truths about God's love and value for us is also true for everyone. God loves every person you see. God designed them with great value and yearns for them to come near to Him, too. God sees their challenges and wounds along with gifts and goodness He placed within them long ago. People are at different places of discovery and some may be at a place where they don't know it's true yet.

As we treasure the delicate way God draws us to His love, we can imagine God carefully tending to another person's need for Him, too. As we talk with them or share time with them, let's share the love we're discovering from God by how we respond to them or encourage them. He loves them as He loves you.

God wants to reset us from the inside and help us with on our skewed outside impression of who we are. We find solid ground and a safe place to rest peacefully when our eyes shift away from all the many outside influences impacting our views of God and ourselves. When we start by welcoming God's truth into our hearts, we can find peace that resides inside because it's God's true peace. It's God's unchanging love for you and His unchanging value existing in every part of you. This is God's reset, and it is solid, trustworthy, and filled with the love and power of God. He doesn't change His mind about you. Others do, but God never will. God loves you no matter what.

Love of the Savior

We Live to Tell How He Loves Us
Women Traveling with Jesus and Disciples
Matthew 27:55-56; Mark 15:41; Luke 8:1-3

The gravel under their feet crunches as the group walks the uneven terrain near the bottom of the path. The Galilean heat of the day intensifies. A town is just ahead. The group of men and women traveling with Jesus have been walking for some time, stepping closer to the next place of miracles. The women enjoy walking together, talking along the way.

"Joanna, do you miss Herod's palace?" Susanna wonders aloud as she wipes the moisture from her face.

With a gentle smile, Joanna glances at her new dear friend, then back to their view ahead.

"Perhaps the beauty. I miss my husband, even though he's quite busy with managing the royal household. I suppose it's restful. Nothing compares to this though," Joanna says pointing forward to the city and to Jesus just steps ahead of them. She adds, "This. This is a different beauty and rest," pressing her hand over her heart. "What Jesus did for me and what He does for each of us, I couldn't bear sitting in Herod's palace. I wanted to help. I wanted to witness it all."

Next to Joanna is Mary Magdalene, who turns the conversation slightly. Mary says, "Susanna, when Jesus healed you, what did it feel like?"

Susanna's weariness disappears from her face as the memory recorded in her mind replays.

"I had been sick for so very long. We heard about Jesus," she begins as her nostalgic eyes watch the back of Jesus leading the group toward the town ahead. "I was desperate, like all of us who come to Him. Waiting. Hoping. Longing to be well. I waited with hundreds of others. Then, there He was. I thought about what I'd say, but I couldn't speak. But I knew He knew. Did you have that? In His eyes, you just feel His complete kindness and He knows everything inside of you. You know He sees you, but in this deeply helping way."

Johanna knowingly nods as Mary responds, "Yes. The kindness. That's what I remember."

Susanna continues, "And that moment when He gently touched my arm, there was warmth. Right away, I was different. I had no pain. Never again." Her thoughts linger as she touches her arm again. "I was whole."

Turning to Mary, Susanna asks, "Mary, you had spirits in you. What was it like for you?"

"Evil spirits are like these horrible thoughts that are just stuck to you. More than that. Deeply attached. And my mind could never find peace," Mary tries to explain. "I was angry all the time and I would yell bizarre things. And voices, so many voices. It was like living in a strange fog all the time and I couldn't escape. The spirits kept pressing on me.

So many people had hurt me over time and the inside of me got darker and darker. It was evil torture every day. Like a disease but it's hard to see."

Joanna wraps her arm around Mary. "I'm so thankful Jesus took them all away for you. You are a precious woman. I love that you're with us now."

Laying her palm over Joanna's hand on her shoulder, she squeezes it. With her other hand she wipes the tear trickling down her cheek.

Mary adds, "It's why I travel with Him, too. It's why we all do. Jesus forever changes us. He heals us to our very core. For me He saved my life."

"He saved me, too," echoes Joanna.

"Me too," Susanna says.

And the voices of some of the other women supporting Jesus and the twelve say together, "He saved us too.

Love of the Savior

Jesus Heals and Feeds
Matthew 15:29-39; Mark 8:1-10

Jesus was walking beside the sea of Galilee. He went to the side of the mountain and sat down. Then crowds began to form. Family and friends. Parents and children. They draw closer, moving toward Him. Groups of beleaguered people caring for others and traveling to find Jesus. It's hope that brings them. It's hope for the lame and crippled they carry with them. Still others lovingly guide those who are blind. So many others press forward with every step that is a difficult challenge.

The crowds come near to the mountain where Jesus sits. They begin to put the lame, the blind, the crippled, the mute, and many others at the feet of Jesus.

And He heals them. One by one. The crowd watches as Jesus causes the mute to speak. The crippled become healthy. The lame walk. The blind ones can see. The crowd calls out and gives glory to the God of Israel.

The day continues to press forward as every person brought to Jesus is healed by Him. The desperate crowd stays to be healed. They stay to watch and listen. Days pass, but Jesus continues to care for the weak and needy.

Love ~ Value ~ Purpose

As the third day begins to reach sunset, Jesus turns to His disciples.

"I have compassion on the crowd because they have been with me now three days and have nothing to eat. And I am unwilling to send them away hungry, lest they faint on the way," Jesus says.

Then, as Jesus had done in a previous place, He turns very little food into a miraculous and satisfying meal for all. He directs the crowd to sit down on the ground. He takes seven loaves and a few fish. He gives thanks, breaks each loaf, and gives it to the disciples to pass to the crowd.

There are 4000 men as well as their wives and children. The vast groupings of joyful and healed people eat. All of them eat and are satisfied. The seven loaves and a few fishes fed everyone and left seven full baskets remaining.

The people were fed, and their bodies all healed.

Only then did Jesus get into a boat to travel to a new region to heal more people. He had cared for all who had come to Him with His compassion and love.

9

Love & Value: Forgiveness

God loves you so much. He created the world for you to see His love. God sees His great value in you and hopefully you are beginning to believe it's true too. In this journey to let these truths change us, we can get even closer to God's heart because Jesus made a way with the Holy Spirit helping us from the inside.

Since God loves you so much, He also doesn't like the way you were hurt by others. He doesn't like when it stays inside of you and causes more harm with each passing day. These are wounds to someone He dearly loves — you.

The only way to finally rid ourselves of the leftover poisons pushed on us . . . is to forgive. This can be so very difficult. Often, we convince ourselves that it's important to hold onto the anger of what was done to us because our minds believe it prevents those who cause harm from getting away with it.

The more we think about it and hold onto it, the more damage it actually does. That's why God asks us to forgive people. It's not so those who injured us can get away with it. It's really for those of us who were hurt. It probably doesn't make human sense, at least not yet.

God knows the damage it does to you when we relive all of it over and over and over. Replaying the images and repeating hurts and emotions — that's where the destruction grows. All the damage and poison goes deeper and deeper. To release those toxins, we can forgive.

Let's line this up with our discussion about pressing out the bad and replacing it with the love and goodness of God. Returning to God's love, value, and purpose helps. We see God's love and beautiful wonders around us and within us. We're thankful for His imprint on this world and our lives. God shows us His heart and compassion by how He interacts with people in the Bible and increasingly we see it in our life. The Savior Stories you've been reading in this book reveal God's love for all people, especially those wounded or trapped by hurtful things.

Then, Jesus laid down His life for every single bad choice ever made because He loves each of us. God uses His same power to heal your wounds that He used to raise Jesus to life and to defeat the effects of evil. God pushes out evil intentions by overpowering it with His love for you.

Let's think about this a little more. What would make evil most pleased? A traumatic event or the event plus an ongoing replay of the emotional and physical harm designed to increasingly hurt you. Satan delights in digging your pain deeper and deeper. It's harder to heal from it that way. When we keep reliving it, we help evil.

Instead, what if you cry out to God and ask Him to help your pain? What if you come close to God and feel His love for you? Can you let God comfort you, weep with you, and gently guide you out of the pain?

Would you rather put yourself in a place where you ask God to bring peace to your pain and restore good inside of you, or would you like to wait for the images and pain to keep returning again. Are there other ways? Yes, but they have limits. We seek counseling, therapy or encouragement from others who try to help with our wounds. Those helping efforts can bring us closer to feeling more whole. However, the resolution never fully comes. It can't. That's because God wants to bring us close to Him so that His beautiful, loving Creator-ability can truly remove the toxins, to comfort you from the damage and to bring life to the wounded parts of you. God's counseling frees us from the traps of evil that will always seek to harm you.

Remember, evil wants to devour you. God wants to free you.

Let's pause to recognize and acknowledge horrible evil done to multitudes of people. I've experienced some, but far less than others. I don't want to gloss over serious injuries. I suspect some wounds still hurt deeply and we shouldn't pretend it was okay.

What I'm indicating about forgiveness is not saying what happened is okay. What I am saying is that God loves you and sees the many sins, hurts and wounds inflicted on you by so many people. He is also powerful enough to get rid of the pain it continues to inflict on you.

Forgiveness frees you. It begins your healing. This does not address consequences and justice for those individuals who commit crimes or abuse or other physical injuries. Nor does it address how we reconcile or reestablish trust in severely broken relationships. God helps with that too.

But first, this is about removing damage done to you in a way that brings healing. God loves you and wants to heal you first. God doesn't walk away from what was done to you. It's like a first responder in medical emergencies. It's crucial to stabilize the person but to also have an underlying purpose toward long-term stability. Since God knows every part of your heart, mind and soul, He can divinely bring healing to all of it.

There are books about forgiveness with some having meaningful concepts to consider. However, the one testimony that changed me the most was Jesus Himself. When He was in excruciating pain and about to die on the cross, He looked up to the Father in heaven and said, "Forgive them. They know not what they do."

Jesus knew every injury and every sin of those who were there that day. He knew they would regret what they were doing to Him. Jesus also knew every sin that every person would ever commit. He wanted to forgive anyway. He said those words for you too. God knows everything for all time and that day He offered you total forgiveness.

Then Jesus said, "It is finished." Jesus provided total forgiveness for the world to choose.

Why?

He knows it's the only way to defeat evil and free us to love God the way He made us to love Him.

Jesus did that for us over 2000 years ago. He knew when we would be born and all the mistakes we would make. He knew all the people we would hurt or who would hurt us. And He died for us anyway. God sees all of your life. He never stops loving you. He died for you that day as well. Jesus gave His life and emerged the Divine Victor. For all of us who had no idea how Satan would take our wounds and make them grow more painful and dig deeper to cause more damage. We didn't know how these growing wounds would hurt others around us.

We had no idea.

Jesus knew. He knew how to rescue us from the impact of sin. He forgives because He loves us. It's something Satan cannot do. Forgiveness overpowers the evil because it can't handle goodness and mercy. Remember the lion seeking to devour its prey. Pursuing and attacking is what he does, but God's goodness is our shield against the attack. We forgive because Jesus showed us how to forgive, and it frees us from the influence of sinful and hurtful efforts to harm.

Forgive and it demolishes evil's lies and stranglehold on you. Forgiveness is not agreeing with what happened. It's about breaking the toxic influence and the harm it causes. It cuts off the poisonous cord funneling more injury into our hearts and minds.

God didn't agree with our bad choices or any of the evil that exists in this world. He just made a way to free us from the harm it causes so we can return to loving Him again.

Believing the lies is what entangles us.

Loving God and forgiving others frees us and denies evil any access to us.

While there are people who understand the harm they inflict, many are acting out of evil and injury done to them. It doesn't excuse it because we know God takes it so seriously that He sent His Son to die as the way to rescue us from it. So, what happened to these people matters to God too. God loves all of us and provides an opportunity for His forgiveness of every single bad choice or hurtful behavior of ours, whether wretched or minimal. Those hurtful people suffered many injuries too. The destructive pain grew inside of them deeply and it spewed out onto you.

Forgiveness is God's extension of His heart for you. He sees our whole story and how He created the person He loves. He sees the value that's waiting to be seen by the person He created. For us, cutting off Satan's hold on us frees us to experience God's love, value, and purpose more fully. For those who injure, God sees the many opportunities He will give them to turn to the magnificent love and forgiveness of God as a way to push away the evil they believe. A life that truly fills with the love and goodness of God is better for everyone. It shuts down another source of evil in the world.

God's great love fills hearts and minds and washes away sins and wounds of our past. Let's look at a contrast of God and evil.

The good we experience from God is love, joy, peace, patience, kindness, goodness, faithfulness, gentleness, compassion, and so much more.

Harm we experience from Satan is envy, anger, fits of rage, idolatry, wrath, slander, malice, greed, and so much worse.

Forgiveness frees us to fully experience amazing facets of God, and it stops evil trying to keep you trapped.

Let's look at a possible situation. Someone does or says something hurtful to you and it's not easy to forget. You're hurt and you keep replaying it. At first, you're just trying to understand what happened and the emotions you're feeling. You're processing the shock of it all.

Then, time passes, and you keep thinking about it and reliving the hurt. When you hear their name or see them, you likely don't get more peaceful about it either. It can play out in your mind multiple ways but here are a few.

Anger at Them: You're mad at them because you didn't deserve what they did to you. They haven't even said they're sorry. They act like nothing happened.

Blaming Yourself: You start to get upset with yourself believing you deserved it or caused it somehow. It's so shocking that you decide it was probably your fault anyway and now you're mad at you. This form of self-blame is common. It's a twisted way we wrongly calculate value and worth.

Combination: This can become anger that they made you feel bad about yourself, even though you've decided you did deserve it somehow. Again, outside, bad circumstances begin to shape our inside view of what happened.

Notice who we did not involve in the conversation?

God.

Further, these types of thoughts cause us to continue to experience the harm in bigger and deeper ways. One problem is that this never stays inside. You may think it does, but it will show up in some way. Our minds get creative. You may start to harm yourself with your thoughts or choices. You might begin to let that anger roll out onto others, harming them. If you let the harm done to you remain unresolved, it will impact you and those closest to you. This doesn't minimize the injury done to you. It actually warns us that it can make the damage even bigger. It has lasting effects and continues to grow unless we realize what's happening.

When we recognize what's happening, we can do what we've been learning. OPEN your heart to God. Talk to Him. Choose God. Pursue Him. Read His Truth in the Bible. Cry out to God for help and to rescue your wounded heart. Call out to Him asking to guide you out of the emotional chaos.

So, what about the person on the other side of the situation? The one who causes the injuries likely has leftover toxins of hurt already deep within them. We're trying to get rid of hurtful effects in our hearts, but they already have something in their hearts that's spilling out on us. In their thoughts, they might try to justify their behavior in some way. Perhaps they don't even think they did anything wrong. Then, really far on the bad side, is someone who enjoys inflicting damage to someone.

Love & Value: Forgiveness

No one starts out this way. Like the poison that can grow inside of us, theirs grew and grew and grew. For them, it may have been encouraged by others around them or brutally inflicted on them. Their toxins gush out into your life and bring great harm to you.

Hurting others can become a serious problem. It tends to be gradual and oftentimes passed on through generations of injury. Remember the human cycle we described earlier. It can also be simple attitudes of disrespect or seeing people as if they don't really matter. The evil lies behind it come from the same source and we can be aware of it.

All of it is built on a great big lie. It's not a new lie. Satan uses the same lie over and over in slightly different ways in each of our circumstances. For some, it's horrible and tragic events, for others it can be over-performing to prove your value and worth through success or accomplishments. In the Garden of Eden, Adam and Eve decided to believe the lies of Satan over loving and believing God. Even Satan tried to tempt Jesus in the desert. Satan declared he would give Jesus all the kingdoms He could see. Jesus would just need to bow down to him. Satan wanted Jesus to choose a lie over loving and believing God.

That's why forgiveness is such an extraordinarily unexpected way to rid our lives of evil attempts to harm us. Not forgiving keeps us trapped in the lie. We can get so out of step with God's love, value, and purpose for our lives that we make horrible choices and injure others. The evil one takes our bad choices and twists them. He tries to cause as much damage as possible. God is willing to help us understand what's happening and replace it with goodness and peaceful comfort.

Love ~ Value ~ Purpose

God doesn't take kindly to this harm of His beloved ones He created. Jesus showed us the unexpected and powerful way to defeat evil for eternity but also in our everyday lives. The power rests in believing God over believing a lie. To believe God, we can look at what Jesus did. He took all of the injuries and said they don't understand it and I still forgive them. Jesus defeated darkness with the goodness and love of God. Evil and Satan cannot love, so they try to deceive and harm us. Unfortunately, it works more than it should.

But now we know more truth and how to see it, defeat it, and keep it outside of our hearts. We choose God inside of us, not the predators trying to get in.

Jesus is the One who died for all sin and forgave everyone. We don't have to do that (Whew!). What He did show us is that we can forgive those injuries that happen to us. The good news is that He didn't leave us to do this all alone. The Holy Spirit of God can live within us and God himself can help us understand how to forgive. God offers us His power to remove evil, hate, anger, bitterness and unforgiveness. The power and truth of the Holy Spirit combined with God's wisdom in the Bible is how it happens.

We can let God push back the power of darkness in our lives and all the toxic ways it's poisoned us. We remember God loves us and created us with His value. We're designed to love God, love others, and love ourselves as He sees us. The toxic poison that repeats the injuries keeps us from feeling the freedom and deep joy of experiencing life with God that He desires for us.

Jesus stretched out His arms on that cross saying, "Forgive them. They know not what they do." It's true. We didn't know, but now we do. This sacrificial love and goodness are what we experience as we spend more time with God. As we do, we'll notice our hearts are different. We begin to see ourselves and the people in our days through God's eyes and something changes in our thoughts about others and how we talk to people. We'll discover fewer and fewer ways we hurt people with our words. When we do speak in a way that's not as loving and gentle as the way God speaks to us, we can tell God we're sorry and say the same to those we've injured. God is quick to forgive those who love Him. He knows you enjoy His goodness pulsing through you rather than the toxic residue of bad choices or hurtful words.

Let God love you in this way.

As our hearts become more thankful for God's love and value for us and for every person, we can practice including those who injure us. We've described love and value as re-setting how we see God and understanding how He sees us. We can try to look at individuals through His eyes and not our own. We may not know all the reasons for their toxins or why they chose to hurt us instead of finding healing with God. But God does, and He loves each of us. We can trust God is working with their hearts and letting them see the hurt they caused. It may not be as quickly as we'd like, but we can begin to trust God.

Forgiveness doesn't happen automatically, but we don't do it alone. God will help us forgive the person who hurt us. It's not your human drive or will to forgive that will change your heart. God wants to do this with you. Imagine Jesus with you, forgiving you. Remember His great love for you that day on the cross and ask Him to put that same love in your heart for those who hurt you. To begin to forgive, this prayer below may be helpful for you.

Please speak this out loud. Our spoken words make an impact on our hearts.

∽

God, you love me and you're changing my heart. Please change my heart a little more and help me to forgive.

Thank you for seeing my pain because You love me.

Thank you, Jesus, that You died for the injury done to me.

Please remove and heal the leftover wounds that stay as unforgiveness, bitterness or simply being unable to stop thinking about it. I'm so sorry, but I didn't know how to let go of it.

I forgive _____ because You love me.

I forgive _____ because You love them.

Love & Value: Forgiveness

God, please fill my heart with Your love and forgiveness for _____.

Please show _____ Your love for them and how to be free from what's hurting them.

Thank you, God. I love You.

Love of the Savior

For All He's Done for You
Weeping Woman Wipes Jesus' Feet
Luke 7:36-50

A religious leader asked Jesus to eat with him, so he joined him for a meal. A gathered group reclines at a table for dinner. In a side room, a quiet, elderly woman gathers more food, but she's really waiting for someone else. She doesn't want her friend to miss it. Then finally, a younger woman with long dark hair and a scarred face scurries in through the archway.

Nearly breathless, she says, "Is He here?"

Nodding to her friend, she asks, "What did you bring?" as she looks at the alabaster jar in her hands.

"I bought this beautiful perfume oil. It's so pure. It's perfect," she says with excitement. "I know it's very, very expensive, but it's for Jesus."

Martha's eyes grow wide, and a hesitant smile begins to lift. "What do you mean for Jesus?" she says, seeking answers to her confusion.

"I don't know exactly. I just know I'm supposed to bless Him with it." She's eager, but also trying to convince herself that what she feels she has to do was actually what she was supposed to do.

The elder woman of the two sets the tray down and asks to hold the jar. Opening the seal, she breathes in the scent of the oil and lets it linger in her senses. "This is so lovely," she says and then returns the alabaster jar of expensive oil. She pauses intently, holding the younger woman's hands and gaze, "Yes. You shall be the one to do this."

They lock eyes, then inhale one more deep breath. As the woman marked with a scar lets her breath out, she turns to enter the room where the men recline at the table.

When she walks in, she sees Jesus. Even though she had seen Him many times, this was different. She had a very certain task. The enormity of blessing Him struck her unexpectedly. She tries to recover. Silently she says, "You overwhelm me Lord, that you would allow a woman like me to be in Your very presence. Steady me God."

The effort to contain her emotions is futile. She begins to remember the healings and majesty of what Jesus had done for her and so many others. Reliving the magnificent ways of Jesus that she had seen and experienced, she begins to weep with humbling thankfulness. Deeply, grateful weeping.

Her stream of tears goes unnoticed at first. She stands behind Jesus and now her weeping will not stop. Overwhelmed again, she kneels to the floor and begins to wipe Jesus' feet with her tears.

Without thinking, she pulls down her hair to better clean his feet. The lowly task of wiping feet didn't matter to her. She wants to cry out, "Thank you Lord for all you've done,"

Love ~ Value ~ Purpose

but she could not. Not in this place. So, she keeps wiping and weeping.

She remembers the seven demons who tormented her and how Jesus effortlessly removed them. Even through the tears, she remembers the oil she felt she had to bring. Opening the jar, she releases the fragrance and begins placing the expensive oil on Jesus' feet.

The One so very worthy of the expense and servant act. With a deeply grateful her heart, she says to herself, "Oh Lord God, anything for you Lord, anything. No matter the cost. You're worth everything."

Some of the men at the table begin to notice, becoming uncomfortable at the scene and powerful aroma filling the air. They scold her.

"Woman, stop. Don't waste that perfume," someone says to her.

But their remarks pass by her, even as some think so little of her. God had seen her, had compassion on her, and healed her. She wanted to thank Him. She was supposed to put this oil on Him, even if she didn't understand why.

Now, even her weeping seems to press back images of the frowns and grimaces, then she hears the Lord defend her.

Jesus turns toward the woman, but speaks to the religious leader who invited him. "Do you see this woman? I entered your house; you gave me no water for my feet, but she has wet my feet with her tears and wipes them with her hair. You gave me no kiss, but from the time I came in, she has not ceased to kiss my feet. You did not annoint my head with oil, but she has anointed my feet with ointment."

With tear-stained face, the woman pauses as she listens to Jesus. Through her wet eyes, she looks up to see His face of compassion looking at her, even as He continues to speak to the others.

"Therefore, I tell you, her sins, which are many, are forgiven. For she loved much. But he who is forgiven little, loves little." Then, speaking to the woman eagerly listening and watching all that He says and does, she hears Jesus say, "Your sins are forgiven. Your faith has saved you; go in peace."

As if frozen by her emotions and the glaring eyes in the room, she stays near Jesus' feet, unable to rise or look at the others. God's forgiveness didn't quickly remove the pain or shame from others. With stillness in the room and not knowing what to do, she continues to wait and listen for Jesus. An uncertainty is growing inside of her.

Then, as if Jesus knows what she's thinking, He says to her, "Your sins are forgiven, and your faith has saved you. Go in peace."

The simple declaration filled with an effortless and authoritative love from the Son of God releases all the pressure of the moment. The intensity in the room lifts. She doesn't turn to look at the other faces in the room who have been humbled by Jesus. The woman simply stands. She bows her head toward Jesus briefly, smiling, and whispers, "Thank you, Lord Jesus."

As the once tormented woman slowly walks toward the doorway to leave the room, the peace He declares for her is filling her body like a water well. The words Jesus spoke over her are changing her. She doesn't understand how the words of blessing, forgiveness and peace could make her feel any different, but somehow, Jesus' words have a power beyond that of any man.

It's the power to heal her sins and wash away the sting of shameful stares judging her. The words of Jesus have the power to touch every part of who we are. He can change how we see everything.

10

Purpose: Designed by Your Creator

So how do we move forward embracing and experiencing God's presence and still feel like we matter in this life? The joys, gifts, and talents that God places in us point to His value and how we were created. What do we do with all of that in a way that is not a "to do" item but living out our individual purpose? How are we to live out this life on earth among the realities of human days? We need to eat. God designed us that way. We're not meant to always be alone. He designed us to relate to other people, whether family or groups of people in our lives.

We're not meant to just sit and do nothing. God chose this time in history for us to be here. Why? How do we navigate all the many other details of experiencing our time on earth before heaven?

God loves us and chose us, so God has a reason for that choice. If you're young, how do you decide the direction for college or a career? If you're retiring, how will you spend your time? What if you're working and suddenly just wondering if there's something else for me?

This is a challenge. It means that we have to be close enough to the Lord that we recognize His voice. It means we have to sit still long enough to hear how He sees us in specific ways. The good news is that we've already begun experiencing God. We're already getting good at noticing God, even going deeper because we want to know Him. We've begun to spend time with Him quietly talking to Him and reading the Bible. This is the place where we've been learning to recognize His voice and how He thinks. Another clear way to get closer to God is by His Spirit.

The Holy Spirit is God. Yet, He's here on earth and inside those who believe in Him. The Holy Spirit is a wonderful Counselor. Just as the Holy Spirit can reveal parts of the Bible that matter to our hearts, He can also lead you toward God's vision for how He designed you.

The truth is that God knows why a certain person likes certain things or is drawn to different interests or curiosities. The Bible is not going to tell somebody whether they should pursue studies in the medical field or be an artist or any other particular profession. We can't point to a verse in the Bible that says, "Be an engineer if you have these five traits." But the Bible does say that we are to ask God for wisdom, and He will grant it generously. We can ask God because He will show us what He wants us to know.

To hear what the Holy Spirit says, we have to spend time learning how to recognize His voice. If a stranger calls you on the phone, you're not going to tell him intimate details of your heart. If you have a dear friend that you trust, you can be vulnerable with them and you are more likely to share personal details.

What do we do? First, we remember that we're believing a true understanding of the love of God, His love for us and His love for humanity. We're practicing this reset of our hearts and minds by opening ourselves to God, looking for Him in our days, and learning the heart and sound of God in the Bible.

We're beginning to look at ourselves and our lives in the loving way God sees us. We have the attitude of discovering what God knows rather than letting others describe our purpose for us. Through God's heart and eyes, we can more wisely understand outside information. That knowledge can also relate to how God made us, such as identifying talents, spiritual gifts and interests. There are many "tests" that can highlight these for you. Many of these are mostly accurate, but often incomplete, so our filter and attitude make a difference.

Personally, I've taken many personality and gift inventories. The gifts tests for me generally come out the same. Interestingly, the personality test changed significantly from when I didn't have faith and when I was new to it as well. Many years later and letting God shape my heart, I can see how all those years masked the person God knew was there.

Something also happened with the gifts tests. God showed me two gifts that I knew showed up on every test, but He also showed me that He gave me another. It was one that usually landed at the bottom of my list of spiritual gifts. God put something in me that I didn't see in myself. When I answered the questions, I must have missed seeing that part of myself. But God knew it was there and He's the One who showed it to me. I offer this as an example of how well-trained and faithful servants of God who develop many of these tests still don't have all the answers we seek. They have wonderful insights to understand pieces of the picture, but God can show you fully His vision for your life.

For you, God wants to reveal His loving plan for the precious person He created. The only way to truly know your individual purpose for this moment in time is to let the Creator of the world share it with you. Perhaps that sounds big and vague or something you just can't do.

You can and it's worth it. It relieves the stress of wondering about that missing something inside of you. God wants to show you. You just have to be willing. When you discover more about how He created you, you'll be so thankful that you get to live the life you were destined to live.

Sometimes our individual purpose can get foggy or off track. Perhaps we hide from a shame by distracting ourselves. Perhaps we don't think we're worthy enough to make an imprint on this world so we pursue what people say we're good at or should do. We step forward into what we think we should do but end up feeling like we've missed something. These can be good and kind commitments for the benefit of others. It can also be filling our time with "growing" a group of real friends or virtual "friends." Sometimes it's destructive to ourselves and to others over time. Other times it can feel rewarding. Accolades, accomplishments, "likes" and other ways the world can recognize that we matter, in their eyes at least. Yet, something still feels missing.

Are we discovering who we are and what we like, or are we letting others' interests guide how we define who we are?

These efforts can get foggy because there are many ways that good people sincerely try to help us discover God's purposes for our life. Many times, this can result in true discovery for how God designed us. These authentic efforts point to spiritual gifts, talents and abilities, with others describing our personalities or temperaments. These tools can help us uncover true information and particular imprints of God's hand in our life. It can also remind us of God's individual and special care for you. His personal touch in you.

What's missing?

The difficulty is that God also has something to say to you about how He designed you. Similar to my experience, this does not show up in our "tests," even though inventories can be quite helpful. Also, the concern is how we think about the results. Does it support the truth that God gave you these gifts and you're discovering them? Or is it a self-driven knowledge to be a better, more successful you? Is it a discovery of other people's ideas of you? Do we look at the results and compare it with praise or rejection we've experienced with people we know? Are we disappointed because we didn't "get a gift" that we think we want? These may seem like petty details, but it's how we understand outside information that matters.

This is similar to our discussion of outside influences trying to define our inside even though our greatest joy and peace comes from God revealing our inside that He made.

God holds the original plan for you. Sometimes, we try to figure it out, but we often can't get all the details to really fit. We can waste so much time being confused and analyzing what others think. From my experience, God put something in me that I didn't see, and others didn't notice. The best part of it though was beginning to wonder how God sees His gifts in me.

We can ask God, "What do you want to do with this gift?" He created it and put it in you, "What's Your plan for it, God?"

The inventories can and do provide insights but please understand them through God's heart first. Sit quietly with God. If you took the tests, ask God what He thinks. How does He see that in your life? What does He want to do with what He gave you? What does God see that you don't, or the tests missed?

Also, please don't run out and sign up for a new activity because it fits the "gifting" description. Sit with God and wonder about it with Him. It settles all the uncertainty and confusion. Even if the answer isn't clear right away, there will be a peace in knowing God will show you in a way that makes sense to you. God wants to strengthen those gifts for your blessing and for others to know His great love. God wants to share that experience with you. It's God's personal touch. In these experiences, He builds your relationship with Him. Keep looking and listening for how He sees you enjoying the gifts He gave you.

God loves you. God values you. God has a purpose for you. The Creator of the earth and the heavens designed you. He thought about you and He has always loved you. We may not see it or understand it at times, but He wants our hearts to see His love first and carry that through everything we see. God wants to experience that with you because He loves you. We don't have to pursue every possibility to try to understand who we are. God created you and wants to show you exactly who you are. The way the world describes you is oftentimes not at all what He sees. God placed in you abundantly more extraordinary qualities than you can imagine.

Look at the wondrous beauty of this earth. It is so complicated yet so beautiful. It's when we look closely that we discover all of the amazing details God put into His big display. It's one thing to look at the vast beauty of the mountains, but it's another to discover what it's made of and how it exists in its ecosystem. It has multitudes of nuances and order required to create and maintain it. Or we can look at the expanse of the ocean and the seemingly endless view. It's simply beautiful, but extraordinarily complicated and powerful.

God loves powerfully and endlessly in the same way He created the natural wonders of the earth. It's in the complicated details of who you are that we discover how God saw all our complicated details fitting together. Ponder the wide range of scientific categorizing of species, personalities, and our intrinsic and microscopic parts as people. These are merely discoveries of the order God put in place long ago. God spoke, then it all came into being. He didn't have to study it because He created it. Humanity has the joy of uncovering and discovering it. You are part of this great discovery.

So, what better way to discover who you are than to go directly to the One who created you? Yes, many resources reveal and point to what God already put in you and that's not a bad thing. The great treasure is letting the Creator show it to you in His unique and long-ago-designed kind of way. A personal, inside informational tour of what's really going on inside of you, the one He loves.

Start with God. Start with the One who created you. Start with the One who saw all the complicated details and how the extraordinary treasure of you fits together.

God's Words Encourage and Guide

"The Lord your God is in your midst, a mighty one who will save; He will rejoice over you with gladness; He will quiet you by His love; He will exult over you with loud singing."
— Zephaniah 3:17

"I have loved you with an everlasting love;
I have drawn you with loving kindness."
— Jeremiah 31:3 (NASB)

"Come near to God and
He will come near to you."
— James 4:8 (NIV)

"We continually ask God to fill you with the knowledge of His will through all the wisdom and understanding that the Spirit gives."
— Colossians 1:9 (NIV)

"If any of you lacks wisdom, you should ask God, who gives generously to all without finding fault, and it will be given to you. But when you ask, you must believe and not doubt, because the one who doubts is like a wave of the sea, blown and tossed by the wind."
— James 1:5-6 (NIV)

"And you also were included in Christ when you heard the message of truth, the gospel of your salvation. When you believed, you were marked in Him with a seal, the promised Holy Spirit."
— Ephesians 1:13 (NIV)

"When the Spirit of truth comes, He will guide you into all the truth."
— John 16:13

"Little children, you are from God and have overcome them, for He who is in you is greater than he who is in the world. They are from the world; therefore, they speak from the world, and the world listens to them."
— 1 John 4:4-5

Love of the Savior

Healed and Designed to Live
Peter's Mother-in-law
Matthew 8:14-17; Mark 1:30-36; Luke 4:38-41

"I'm so hot," she thinks as she lay weak in her bed. The fever had lingered all day. In her fogginess of mind, she remembers, "Peter's coming home today. He's bringing Jesus. Oh, I wanted to make everything special for them. All the food I prepared...If only..."

Sleepiness interrupts her thoughts. She only feels heat all over her body and her thoughts make no sense to her.

In the doorway leading to the other room, she can see the front entrance. Her eyes burn as she blinks, trying to focus. "I wonder if they were coming today," she tries to remember. "I don't know. Oh, I can't think very well." Her lethargic body lays in the heat of the fever.

Then, she hears men talking as they approach the house. A meager, weak smile comes on her face. She sees others in Peter's house welcome the men. One of them turns His head in her direction. She feels joy in her heart and tries to ignore the heat of her body's fever. She can see Jesus' eyes just over the head of another person. The piercing eyes of kindness. Her weak body is still, but even through her fog of sickness she can see Jesus. He begins to walk over to her, but with groggy thoughts, she struggles to focus.

There are no lengthy words or displays. Jesus keeps His eyes on her with every step He takes. She knows that He sees her filled with a fever. He doesn't speak, but to every part of her existence, she hears His peaceful pursuit of her.

Jesus stops. He looks down upon her weary body, unable to rise and pressed down by the fever. His eyes do not leave hers.

Then, a gentle touch of His hand.

The fever leaves her.

An instantaneous moment of total release from heat, lethargy, aches, weariness and sickly weightiness.

All of it is gone.

As gently as He came, He quietly walks back to the group within Peter's house.

Peter's mother-in-law was filled with more than healing from her fever. She has joy. She has energy. Her mind is clear, and her body is more than well. All she had wanted to do was to care for the traveling group. Now she can.

She rushes to gather food and helps those already baking. She quickly brings it to Jesus and the others.

"My Lord, for you. I prepared it for you," she says.

Jesus thanks her and smiles with kind eyes. He knows her delight.

Her thoughts are filling her mind and bringing an overwhelming joy to her heart. Jesus had seen her and knew

Love ~ Value ~ Purpose

how she had prepared for His arrival. He healed her and gave her the gift of loving Him in return. Just the way she wanted.

The family members who had been in the house with her for days, look at her as she brings plenty of food for everyone. Their thoughts are the same. "How is she suddenly well?"

But then they remember Jesus. As He entered the house, He took a barely noticed turn. It was so brief that many missed it as they welcomed the traveling group.

"He must have healed her fever," one whispers to another as they exchange knowing glances and nods.

As the evening continues, Jesus heals many more bodies and lives that night. Many knew of Jesus and they had brought the sick and those possessed by demons. Jesus healed them all. That evening, family and friends at Peter's house watched as Jesus casted out demons and healed every sick person who came to Him. Each miracle brings joyful, humble amazement to everyone. To those He healed, Jesus delivered so much more.

As she ended her emotionally full day, Peter's mother-in-law sat down. She felt rest, but also thankful excitement. Jesus had taken time to show His love and compassion for her. He healed her, but even more than that, she was able to love on others the way she always loves to do. She rejoiced with all the amazing blessings and miracles that took place that night, including her own.

Truly the Son of God had seen her. His peaceful heart and healing hands made His love and compassion real for all of them.

11

Purpose: Loving Others as God Loves You

God's love, value, and purpose for us can truly change how we see ourselves. When we look through the eyes of a loving, powerful God, His outpouring of love into our hearts and minds can also overflow into our relationships. God's love, value, and purpose begins to change how we relate with others. We begin to have a true love for the individuals in our lives.

Love God with all your heart, mind and soul and love others as yourself (Matthew 22:37-40). This is our human purpose God has for us. So far, we've taken time to embrace our loving God and His love for us. We're learning to love God and enjoy time with Him. We're discovering new insights about Him we didn't know and learning so much about ourselves through His eyes. We're beginning to love ourselves in all the ways God created us uniquely. We're noticing this peaceful difference when we talk with others or spend time with them. But then there may also be times when life and people still feel complicated. The Bible has answers for us, but sometimes we filter it through our human thoughts first. This can cause us to tumble back toward doing what others tell us is the right way or how we should be doing something.

God's heart of love and value is the filter we can remember as a guide for us. God's perspective shows us truth as we read the words He placed in the Bible.

Let me explain. There are many verses, especially in the New Testament, that guide us on how to relate well to others through our interactions and attitudes toward them. However, if we emphasize a heart of love and value, then as we look at these verses, we can avoid performing to do list.

God is not focused on a to do list. He has a heart focus.

For example, we're encouraged to tame our tongues, which simply means be careful what you say. If we look at it from a typical point of view, we may focus on behaving ourselves and doing all that we can to not say gossipy words. This is not a terrible strategy, but it's really a matter of forcing yourself to do something. This works for a while, but it gets hard. We want to do something that's good, so we try our best. Then, we get frustrated when we mess up.

If we approach the same concept using a love, value, purpose heart, this changes how we approach it.

God loves us and loves everyone. He gave each of us great value and wants to protect us. Our purpose is to get to know God and come to love Him, then we can love ourselves and others well. God wants this for everyone.

When we talk about someone in a way that's hurtful, what are we doing? God says He loves you so much and gives you so much value. He also loves and values that person, too.

It's God who loves you and you love Him back. What we say really connects to our relationship with God. When we say harsh words about others it wounds someone God loves. Just as if someone wounded your loved one, it wounds your heart, too.

Perhaps you feel like they don't deserve kind words. Yet, there are times in each of our lives when our behavior is far less than kind as well. The extraordinary part is that God loves us whether we say kind words or don't say kind words. However, He knows the damage the words can cause, but He also doesn't stop loving us when we don't see it from His heart first. God guides us back to seeing situations from His loving perspective. He's loving us and reminding us to love others in the same way. It allows God's love and goodness to thrive instead of harsh, hurtful, or unkind words that cause harm.

What we're learning is that God loves us so much and He knows the precious value in each one of us. He goes to remarkable lengths to show it to you including the death of His own Son. Since God loves you that much and knows everything about everything, then it makes a little more sense to think about how He sees these situations. He knows the damage hurtful choices cause all of us, for the givers of harm and those who receive.

God also knows the story of the person you're describing with your attitude or words. He knows how their story unfolds. He sees the goodness in that person. It's not up to us to say something bad about someone God loves.

Imagine God sitting right there in the room with you. How would He feel about what you're saying? The truth is, God is always there and does see everything. As we love God more and grow in being thankful for how much He loves us, our thoughts won't go as quickly to speaking unkindly about someone He loves. We'll be quick to listen rather than speak. We'll be quick with our compassion and understanding rather than hurting someone with our words.

Let's get more complicated. Say there's a person who is mean to you whenever you're around them. Before you see them, ask God to protect your heart and mind from any hurtful words they might say. Ask God to stop the devil from influencing that person. Also, ask God to keep your heart and mind focused on His view of you. Outside bad influences are not welcomed into our inside.

How do you handle those moments when what they say hurts you? If we apply a love, value, purpose heart to the moment, we can first remember God loves us and we only take in His goodness. The words being spoken don't take away God's love or His value for you. Those words are meant to harm, even if the person saying them doesn't want them to hurt. Harmful words can hurt, whether they come at us intentionally or not. You can say to God silently, which is prayer, "God, please keep these words outside of me. I only want your good things in me."

When you respond, you can remember that God is right there with you, in all His pure, loving, Creator-God bigness. You are greatly loved and valued because the Creator of the earth and heavens declares it to be true. The other person may not see life through God's eyes, but you can remember how God sees you.

If people realized God was in the room, they probably wouldn't behave that way. In the moment, you can also pray, "Lord give me the right words." When you speak, do so with truth that carries kindness, peace, gentleness and patience. These can quickly defuse the situation. This doesn't mean you tell the person their behavior is okay. It just simply means that you acknowledge that what they're saying is hurtful, but you don't yell or say it as retaliation.

If this is a person who regularly acts this way toward you, perhaps you say, "The words you're saying are hurtful. I'm not letting hurtful things into my heart anymore. I'm not sure what you're trying to communicate, but you'll need to find another way to share it with me. I am taking in words that are kind, patient and life-giving."

Remember, God sees the entire situation. You. Them. What's inside each of you. The good news is that if you believe and confess that Christ died for your sins, then the Holy Spirit lives inside of you. It's a mystery how, but it's also very true. It takes practice to remember, but you can.

God treasures you and wants to help you push away the harm that comes to you. Ask for His help. That doesn't mean the matter gets resolved every time. It just means that as you walk through difficult times, you can remember who you are and that you belong to God. No one can take away that truth.

As we've practiced stopping the outside influences that try to reach us inside, this is again similar. These can be harder because it's not as easy as turning off the news. A heart of love, value, purpose is about resting in the truth and reality of God and how He loves you.

When we start by welcoming God's presence on the inside of us, we will begin to more easily handle hard words coming at us. What people say doesn't change who God is, how He sees you, and how much He loves you. The bad things belong on the outside of you. We desire to experience the goodness of God – love, joy, peace, patience, kindness, goodness, faithfulness, gentleness and compassion. If it's not that, then you know what it really is … the big lie trying to get you to believe wicked ideas about you and others.

This also means we reject the ploy to harm others by retaliating. It's not simple. It's not easy. It can take practice. Most of all, it takes listening to the Spirit of God inside of you. He can show you good ways to prepare your heart and to respond at any given moment. You'll also notice that you are changing as God continues to reshape your heart. We begin to hear and see the words of others as the outside things they truly are. This gives us the strength to determine what is the goodness that God wants for us and what's not His goodness.

You're so greatly loved by Him that no matter what, He is always with you. When we struggle, God is right there to encourage and comfort you. So is all His great love and value He's been pouring into you. Sometimes these hard moments are opportunities to realize how much God is changing, rebuilding, and protecting us. Even when we forget all of these truths about God in a moment, He opens His arms to hold us and heal us again when we turn to Him.

The reality is that as we go through life, we will face

difficult situations and difficult people. The more we desire to be guided by God's love for us and His truth in the Bible, the more we will discover treasures of God's wisdom and it will transform us in ways that lets us love others well. The more we love God, the more this will make sense for our love, value, purpose hearts. Our hearts will soften toward others and we'll be more aware of harmful influences. We'll begin to live our lives filtered through God's love and value.

With God's love, He causes us to love others. He is good and He loves well. So, He will lead you beside "still waters" and nourish your soul. He brings gentleness to your heart and your thoughts. God brings joy to your spirit and kindness to your words. He will be with you always and love you always. God has great love for you and is always for you.

Experiencing God's deep transformational love causes our hearts to overflow with the love He's shown us. Our eyes begin to see the wounds of others. Just as He cared for your wounds, He will ask you to share that love with people whose hearts are broken, lonely, or trapped in ways that you've also known. This may be in new relationships with others, or something more organized. It may lead you to new communities, cities, businesses, or even the world. He may send you to third-world poverty-stricken areas or He may call you to love greatly within your home. God's love in us spills out toward loving others, sharing His love, and drawing others to Him ... just like He did for you. In this beautiful journey, you'll be amazed and humbled as you experience the ways God will uncover great and unexpected details and events in your life and relationships that He desires to share with you.

Love ~ Value ~ Purpose

God wants His love to bring joy to your life. He brings comfort and guides you. God offers you peace beyond what you can know or imagine. God fills you with all these good and wonderful experiences of His love and you will want to share that with others. God may take you to places you never imagined, but you will deeply treasure all of God's plans for you.

Love of the Savior

Help and Hope in Despair
Women at the Cross with John
Matthew 27:45-66; Mark 15:33-47;
Luke 23: 44-56; John 19:17-42

The last hour had been excruciating, filled with despair and shock. Jesus' mother, women who had traveled with Him, the disciples and many others had gathered to watch the One who declared the forgiveness of sins and God's kingdom was coming. He was being crucified, and death was near.

Just before He spoke, "It is finished," Jesus looked down at His mother and John, his disciple. "Take this woman as your mother," He had said. Even to the end, He cared deeply for His mother.

When the crucifixion ended, shock immediately came to all those present.

It is recorded this way.

At that moment the curtain of the temple was torn in two from top to bottom. The earth shook, the rocks split, and the tombs broke open. The bodies of many holy people who had died were raised to life. They came out of the tombs after Jesus' resurrection and went into the holy city and appeared to many people.

"When the centurion and those with him who were guarding Jesus saw the earthquake and all that had happened, they were terrified, and exclaimed, 'Surely, he was the Son of God!'"

Tremendous confusion and dramatic divine power were on display at the physical death of the Son of God. Along with the extraordinaty events, those who loved Jesus grappled with intense emotional loss. The body of the One they loved, and Who had loved them, had perished.

His mother began the slow walk down the mountain in despair. With her are Mary Magdalene and Salome. They walk in sorrow and remembering those final moments. Jesus had cried out, "It is finished," then His body went limp.

Now, Mary Magdalene weeps as she presses her arm around Jesus' mother and tries to steady their steps. The ache and sorrow cut to the core of their bodies and the deepest places of their heart.

The Lord had been crucified.

As the women walk and weep, a man comes before Mary, Jesus' mother.

"My name is Joseph of Arimathea. I am a member of the council and I received permission from Pilate to bury your son. I have a tomb where no one has ever laid," he says.

Paralyzed by the tragedy unfolding, the mother stares at the man through her tears.

Mary Magdalene nods to the man, then gently speaks to Mary. "We will go with them. We will care for your Son."

The women watch as Joseph leads the men carrying Jesus, carefully wrapped in linen. Mary Magdalene walks with the women who journeyed with Jesus from Galilee, remembering the many miracles He gave to so many. Mary remembers the demons leaving her at His command and her freedom that came from that moment. Every person who pursued Him received healing.

In the sadness, she recalls His great love for all. The lives He rescued and changed pass through her mind, one after another, then another ...so many that it seems endless. The faces of the desperate men, women, fathers, and mothers hoping Jesus would be all the people said He was... the Son of God. Mary Magdalene knows He truly was, and that Jesus loved every person He saved.

The presence of memories begins to fade, set aside briefly as they approach the tomb. The women follow the man Joseph to a hollowed-out rock cave. An enormous boulder was on the side and some of the men carefully lay Jesus in the tomb. There's a solemn hush. The heaviness in their hearts and thoughts matches the weight of the stone slowly closing access to the One who saved so many.

The next day, the chief priests and Pharisees gather before Pilate. They had remembered Jesus saying He would rise after three days. They plead with Pilate to guard the tomb to prevent the disciples from taking away the body. Pilate tells them to go make the tomb as secure as they can and seal it. They don't want anyone to claim that Jesus had risen from the dead.

Love of the Savior

Women at the Resurrection
Matthew 28:1-10; Mark 16:1-13;
Luke 24:1-12; John 20:1-18

The Lord's body had been laid in the rock tomb. The women and others had returned home as the Sabbath was beginning, ushering in a time of rest. For each of them, it was a strange time of absence from the Lord who had walked among them. Quiet sadness, shock, and confusion. At dawn, while it was still dark, the women rushed out to the tomb with spices prepared for the ceremony.

"Mary, Mary, wait," said Joanna, as she tries to keep close to her friend. "Who will roll away the stone?"

Mary Magdalene briskly scurries ahead toward the tomb.

"We must take our spices to anoint Him," Mary says as they come upon the tomb.

Suddenly, she stops. The other women stop, too. The earth below their feet shakes. When the trembling stops, they look at the tomb.

The stone is rolled away.

The women stare at the open entrance with wonder and confusion. Their emotions and thoughts swirling at possibilities, only to be halted again.

An angel appears to them dressed in a dazzling white robe. The angelic presence transforms the confusion to fear.

Mary, Joanna and the others want to speak, but can only stare. The figure quickens the pace of their hearts and panic is close behind. The clothing is like lightning and he sits effortlessly atop the dense boulder.

"Do not be afraid," the angel says. "For I know you seek Jesus who was crucified, but He is not here. He is risen. Remember how He told you?"

The power of the words ricochets in their minds, feeling true and familiar, but not altogether making sense to them. They saw Jesus die. They watched as His body was placed here.

The angel continues, "Come, see the place where He lay, then go quickly to tell the disciples."

Stepping slowly forward, they gingerly walk into the tomb. The empty tomb. Their eyes dart back and forth, scanning each other and the room-like area. Jesus is not in the tomb.

Immediately, Mary Magdalene turns to the other women, "We must go tell the disciples! He's alive! He did what He said He would do!" Grasping two of the women's arms as she pulls them out of the tomb. "Hurry, we must tell them. It's all true. It's all true!"

The women run as quickly as they can. Mary Magdalene finds the disciples, but only John and Peter believe her. Breathless, she tries to tell them the tomb is empty. Joy in her wispy, exhausted voice. She pulls at them, "Come, come. The tomb is empty."

John and Peter leave quickly. She tries to follow them back to the tomb, but weariness causes her to trail behind. Once she arrives, she sees them stepping out of the tomb. Their faces carry the same confusion she had moments ago.

"The linen is folded, and Jesus is not in the tomb," Peter muffles as Mary steps closer. John and Peter try to understand as they return home, wondering. They didn't yet fully understand what Jesus meant when He said He would rise again in three days.

But Mary Magdalene stays. She lingers in the room where Jesus had lain. She'd been thrilled at what the angel spoke. When she was running, she felt the possibility of celebration. And yet, what now?

She starts to wonder, "Where is the Lord? He said He would rise on the third day, but where is His body? What does this mean?"

The happiness and unknown of these last few days of grief and rest mingle with the many emotions. It all begins to emerge as exhausted, tender tears falling from her eyes and down her cheeks.

Suddenly, brightness begins to create a glow in the room. Mary looks up, but without fear when she sees them this time. Two angels sit at each end of the stone surface where Jesus had lain.

"Why are you weeping?" They speak tenderly to her.

Unsure of how to share the tumbling emotions inside, she says, "They have taken away my Lord and I don't know where they have laid Him." As the last of her words depart her lips, she feels something change in the room. An indescribable something, so she turns around.

Jesus is standing there, but she doesn't recognize Him right away.

He says, "Why are you weeping? Whom are you seeking?"

Her mind is busy shuffling so many thoughts and emotions. Her eyes are unable to see through her tears clearly. She thinks it's a gardener or caretaker.

"Sir, if you have carried Him away, tell me," she says.

Then Jesus speaks again, "Mary."

Immediately, she's able to recognize Him. She falls to His feet to worship the Lord. He was here.

"Do not be afraid. Go tell my brothers to go to Galilee and there they will see me."

Holding the feet of the Savior who rescued her from demons and had compassion on thousands upon thousands of people, she could barely breathe. Overwhelming joy and deep, exhilarating thankfulness pulsed through her body. She trembled with awe and joy.

The Son of Man had rescued people on this earth, then He died for them, too. Now, as only God could do, He rose again. Exactly what He said He would do.

In this moment, Mary, who had lived with demons torturing her very soul, now lived to worship at the risen Savior's feet. Life would never again be the same. For anyone.

Love ~ Value ~ Purpose

12

Love ~ Value ~ Purpose

You are loved by the miraculous powerful God who created glorious and wonderful beauty all around us. His power is great, and it is also greatly personal. Experiencing this for yourself is a journey with moments of unexpected freedom and deeply transforming love. God loves you no matter what. He's right there and He's your first and best encourager. He comes to you with His great personal love.

We don't have to fear this world with all the chaos and anger. We have the greatest power of all, and He defeats lies and hate. We have God and He loves with power that transforms and resettles our hearts in a way that guards and protects from the lies trying to cause harm from a distance or right in front of us.

God is mighty so those who seek to cause us harm should fear the greatness of God. The One who creates can defeat. God creates love and value that is magnificent, pure, and true for every life and even wonders upon this earth and in heaven. The ever-changing world never stops trying to define these ideas on their own and without God. This is the chaos that brings hurt into the world.

Yet, God's love, value and purpose began before any of us ever took a breath, and it is His breath that created it all. This is the One who thought about you long ago, brought you to life, and has already seen all of your days. When we pursue our Creator, we discover who we really are. We discover what real love and value looks like. We can understand how we fit into this life and why God put us here now, for this time in history.

> Remember . . . our Love, Value, and Purpose begin with our Creator.

> **Love.** God created the heavens and earth to display His love for you. God loves His creation and each person whom He individually designs. God wants to reveal that love to you in deeply personal ways and through experiencing your life with Him. God offers to rescue, protect, and guide you with His love.

> **Value.** Out of God's love, He created treasures of great worth. The world He created for us has great value to God. Every person has tremendous value, because He created each one. God knows your true value and wants to help you dis-

cover what that really is. God created you so that your joy is connected to Him. It's meant to draw you to Him so He can reveal the personal treasures He placed within you, but also so He can add even more to your life. Your value is defined by Him and it's deeply important to Him. Through His love, He wants to convince you of His value in you.

Purpose. God loves you and delights over you. He wants to rescue and heal you from great sadness so that you can have His great goodness and peace flowing through you. God loves you, treasures you and has a special, unique purpose for you. To experience this life with Him in all the fullness He intended, you can let God uncover the wonderful ways He designed your life purposes. As we embrace God's love, value and purpose for our individual lives, we begin to share that life with others through the love of God that overflows from within us.

Love . Value . Purpose .

<u>**You**</u>

Love: God loves you.

Value: God values you.

Purpose: God created you with unique and special purposes.

Everyone

Love: God loves all of us.

Value: God values every person.

Purpose: God created everyone with purpose.

Your Life

Your purpose is to love, know, and experience God and His love, value, and purpose in your life, then to share that love with others.

In the journey, God will guide us toward seemingly endless goodness and unexpected treasures, even during our difficult seasons. The closer we are to God and experiencing His love, the more we'll see Him during our everyday lives with people He places in our path. Once you seek God and His wisdom, He promises He will reveal it to you. He will show you how your passion and the ways He created you will bring greater joy for you and for others. This may be right within your family or it may be something that has global impact in the lives of hundreds of thousands of people.

God sees you from the inside and His great love shapes us to make a difference among those outside of us. We can turn away from a life with reverse thinking and be freed from our minds sloshing around with the constant changes in this world. When we let God reset our inside, we can rejoice, be restored, and find stable peace. We can see harm coming toward us and stop it from causing damage. If we miss it, then God is right there to rescue and heal.

We can live in God's love, walking in His peace inside of us, and rejoicing that we are free from those things that try to hurt us. This is what experiencing God's love, value, and purpose in us really looks like.

It's an extraordinary gift to know you are loved and valued by God. He's seen all the days of your life and you bring God joy. God is the Creator of the world and all the amazing details within you. He loves. He protects. He rescues. He guides. He redeems. Then, He loves even more. God will be with you always. You do not have to fear, because Creator God loves you.

When I first learned of God's love, I didn't know much. Then, I read about what Jesus did during a short time He walked on earth. Once I was pretty sure, God brought people in my path so that I could be sure. God walked along with me before I ever spoke and believed Jesus is indeed the Son of God who died for me, and every person, regardless of whether they believe in Him one day.

He doesn't force us to come to Him and believe, but He absolutely comes right to you when you offer Him your heart. God comes right to you as you seek to know Him, to understand who He really is and then offer your heart to be forgiven by Him.

I've walked a long journey with God, and I see how gently and lovingly God carried me forward in His love. I wish I could say I loved Jesus with my whole heart the moment He gave me salvation, but that would not be true. The problem was me. I was so emotionally broken, but God showed me how to be loved by Him and what authentic love really is. I loved God with all that I knew and that was enough for Him. God knew how He was going to let me experience His love as a way to understand love. It was His love that showed me I could deeply love Him and as a result, love others well.

At times I'm overwhelmed when I realize the Creator of the heavens and the earth wanted me to experience His love when I had very little to give. But that little bit of love was all I knew. To God, it was enough. He proved to me that He loved me more than any other person in the world could love me.

Perhaps you wonder if your love is enough. It is more than enough. A tiny little bit of hoping to understand the love of God is what He truly treasures. He understands that it's all you know how to give.

God's love is pure and authentic, patient and nurturing, kind and merciful, redeeming and healing, powerful and passionate. During the many and inevitable human trials, He was with me. Even when I couldn't "feel" Him, I eventually saw how He was there or discovered later how He had been with me.

God will do the same for you. He promises He will. God can let you experience a rich love and encouragement in the Scriptures, through prayer or journaling, and gathering with other others to pursue the heart of God. He desires to give you God-only interactions with Him and individuals who journey through your days. And so much more. God is not limited to our ideas and He knows how to reach each of us in deeply meaningful ways.

I can declare with absolute certainty that when you finally come to a place of being willing to offer God as much of your heart as you know how, He will respond to you. You may not be able to imagine a life of joy, peace, and comfort, but you can have one. That's the way you were created by God and He will create that life for you.

As you began to read about Jesus in this book, hopefully you saw His love and compassion for those cast aside, forgotten, suffering or harmed. He didn't heal every person on earth, but He did heal those who came to Him.

You can go to Him, too. You can say in your mind or out loud:

> "God, You say knock and You will open the door. Jesus, I knock on Your door now and ask You to show Yourself to me. There are so many parts of my life that don't make sense. I'm not sure this makes sense to me either, but I'm going to offer You my heart. I'm asking You to show me You're real. Show my heart so I can know how to believe You love me."

In these moments, if you feel your heart giving way to the truth that Jesus loves you, ask yourself if you believe Jesus is God's Son who died for your sins. God already knows all of our sins, and Jesus did die for every one of them. If you're not sure, pray or say this:

> "Lord, help me to believe you, Jesus, with a true heart. Like the people in the stories, help my unbelief."

If you feel inside that it is true for you, then speak to God out loud. This is important and it will forever change your life now and for eternity.

"Lord God, thank You for sending Your Son Jesus to live a sinless human life and then die for my guilt. It is a gift I don't ever have to repay, and You offer it to me anyway. I agree that I have sinned against You, just as every person in this world has done. I'm so sorry. I had no idea the sadness that sin causes You and others.

"You died for me, Jesus. I believe You wash away my sin and that You are the Lord God. Please lead and guide my life so I can love You more, love others well, and love me as You made me.

"Thank You God, Amen."

Whether God is new to your heart or He simply looks newly magnificent to you, may God's love, joy and peace wash over you in a way that is meaningful and precious to you.

Earlier, I asked you to imagine sitting in a room with God and that He was speaking to you. Perhaps return to the words in Chapter 2 or read this small part to settle into your heart.

Recall the many words of God's great love for you described on these many pages. Breathe in the truth and memory of those words. Now, hear the words of the Lord to you again.

All the people are precious to Him. He forgets not a one. He calls them by name and gifts them with favor and blessing. All the world sees the beauty God gave them. It is for joy, peace, provision, comfort, care, wisdom, and blessing.

> "I do not gift lightly or insufficiently. I am God Almighty who chooses to bring loveliness. My love is great, and many try to cheapen it or lie about it. I am God who greatly loves and gives. I will not be deterred from my people. I love them and I am coming for them. They belong to me and not the evil in this world. I declare My presence will matter to them again.
>
> "Holy, holy, holy. Honor and glory to the Lord. His people shall once again see the goodness of the Lord. I love them and I will come for them."

God's pure love brings joy, peace, provision, comfort, care, wisdom, and blessing. God brings peace, rest, and wholeness through His love, value, and purpose for you.

Experience the wholeness and peace of your love, value, and purpose found in the wonders of God, His Bible and the many ways He shows you His love and rescues your heart, mind, and soul. As you do, you can share and experience God's great love for you with the many individuals He puts in your path as well.

Love. Value. Purpose. God wants to reveal and experience it all with you because He created it just for you. Will you let Him?

Love

Value

Purpose

God loves you.

"I am God Almighty who chooses
to bring loveliness.
My love is great,
and many try to cheapen it
or lie about it.
I am God who greatly loves and gives."

God has come to reveal His love
and to rescue your heart.

Are you ready?

Love ~ Value ~ Purpose

OPEN Your Heart to God

This is a safe space for you to let your heart be embraced by Mighty God who loves you with an everlasting love. Note what God shows you in this precious place with Him.

OFFER Your Heart to God Who Loves You:

PRAISE & PRAYER to God Who Loves You:

EXPLORE & EXPERIENCE God Who Loves You:

NEW PRESENCE & PERSPECTIVES from God Who Loves You:

Notes

Notes

Dedication

God, I am completely Yours. This book is the work of Your love in my life. Through this life journey with You, I became free, more so than I've ever been, and loved more than I could ever imagine possible. Thanking You is not nearly enough and reveals only a fraction of Your love for me and my love for You. I am Yours God, just as I was always meant to be.

May those who read the words in this book feel Your presence and Your heart for them in ways that cause them to experience the deep and wonderful love You have for them.

God, I love You forever.

About the Author

Amy Myers lives in Virginia near Washington, DC with her husband and children. She grew up at the base of the Rocky Mountains, then moved to the rocky world of politics in Washington, DC after college. Happily leaving it behind to raise their family, Amy discovered a deeper love for God, the Bible, and helping women of all ages experience the love of God through Scripture, His Spirit, and community.

As founder of Thy Name, Amy seeks to increase opportunities for authors and artists to publish stories and creative works that God places in their hearts. She also enjoys serving as a prayer intercessor at church and hosting a podcast titled God-cast. She is the author of *Love ~ Value ~ Purpose* and holds a Master of Divinity degree.

Ways to connect with Amy:
www.lovevaluepurpose.com
www.thy-name.com
https://god-cast.podbean.com

Cover Photo & Design: Grace E. Myers